C000150227

Microsoft Certified Azure Fundamentals AZ-900

Practice Questions

Version 1

www.ipspecialist.net

Document Control

Proposal Name	:	Microsoft Certified: Azure Fundamentals Practice Questions
Document Version	:	Version 1
Document Release Date	:	
Reference	:	AZ-900

Feedback:

If you have any comments regarding the quality of this book, or otherwise alter it to better suit your needs, you can contact us through email at info@ipspecialist.net

Please make sure to include the book's title and ISBN in your message.

About IPSpecialist

IPSPECIALIST LTD. IS COMMITTED TO EXCELLENCE AND DEDICATED TO YOUR SUCCESS.

Our philosophy is to treat our customers like family. We want you to succeed, and we are willing to do everything possible to help you make it happen. We have the proof to back up our claims. We strive to accelerate billions of careers with great courses, accessibility, and affordability. We believe that continuous learning and knowledge evolution are the most important things to keep re-skilling and up-skilling the world.

Planning and creating a specific goal is where IPSpecialist helps. We can create a career track that suits your visions as well as develop the competencies you need to become a professional Network Engineer. We can also assist you with the execution and evaluation of your proficiency level, based on the career track you choose, as they are customized to fit your specific goals.

We help you STAND OUT from the crowd through our detailed IP training content packages.

Course Features:

❖ Self-Paced Learning
- Learn at your own pace and in your own time

❖ Covers Complete Exam Blueprint
- Prep-up for the exam with confidence

❖ Case Study Based Learning
- Relate the content with real life scenarios

❖ Subscriptions that Suits You
- Get more and pay less with IPS subscriptions

❖ Career Advisory Services
- Let the industry experts plan your career journey

❖ Virtual Labs to test your skills
- With IPS vRacks, you can evaluate your exam preparations

❖ Practice Questions
- Practice questions to measure your preparation standards

❖ On Request Digital Certification
- On request digital certification from IPSpecialist LTD.

About the Authors:

This book has been compiled with the help of multiple professional engineers who specialize in different fields e.g. Networking, Security, Cloud, Big Data, IoT etc. Each engineer develops content in his/her own specialized field that is compiled to form a comprehensive certification guide.

About the Technical Reviewers:

Nouman Ahmed Khan

AWS-Architect, CCDE, CCIEX5 (R&S, SP, Security, DC, Wireless), CISSP, CISA, CISM, Nouman Ahmed Khan is a Solution Architect working with a major telecommunication provider in Qatar. He works with enterprises, mega-projects, and service providers to help them select the best-fit technology solutions. He also works as a consultant to understand customer business processes and helps select an appropriate technology strategy to support business goals. He has more than fourteen years of experience working in Pakistan/Middle-East & UK. He holds a Bachelor of Engineering Degree from NED University, Pakistan, and M.Sc. in Computer Networks from the UK.

Abubakar Saeed

Abubakar Saeed has more than twenty-five years of experience, managing, consulting, designing, and implementing large-scale technology projects, extensive experience heading ISP operations, solutions integration, heading Product Development, Pre-sales, and Solution Design. Emphasizing on adhering to Project timelines and delivering as per customer expectations, he always leads the project in the right direction with his innovative ideas and excellent management skills.

Areeba Tanveer

Areeba Tanveer is a AWS Certified Solution Architect – Associate working professionally as a Technical Content Developer. She holds a Bachelor's of Engineering Degree in Telecommunication Engineering from NED University of Engineering and Technology. She also worked as a project Engineer in Pakistan Telecommunication Company Limited (PTCL). She has both the technical knowledge and industry sounding information, which she utilizes effectively when needed.

Syed Hanif Wasti

Syed Hanif Wasti is a Computer Science graduate working professionally as a Technical Content Developer. He is a part of a team of professionals operating in the E-learning and digital education sector. He holds a Bachelor's Degree in Computer Sciences from PAF-KIET, Pakistan. He has completed training of MCP and CCNA. He has both the technical knowledge and industry sounding information, which he uses efficiently in his career. He previously worked as a Database and Network administrator and obtained a good experience in software development.

Free Resources:

With each workbook purchased, IPSpecialist offers free resources to our valuable customers.

Once you buy this book you will have to contact us at support@ipspecialist.net or tweet @ipspecialistnet to get this limited time offer without any extra charges.

Free Resources Include:

Exam Practice Questions in Quiz Simulation: With 300+ Q/A, IPSpecialist's Practice Questions is a concise collection of important topics to keep in mind. The questions are especially prepared following the exam blueprint to give you a clear understanding of what to expect from the certification exam. It goes further on to give answers with thorough explanations. In short, it is a perfect resource that helps you evaluate your preparation for the exam.

Career Report: This report is a step-by-step guide for a novice who wants to develop his/her career in the field of computer networks. It answers the following queries:

- What are the current scenarios and future prospects?
- Is this industry moving towards saturation or are new opportunities knocking at the door?
- What will the monetary benefits be?
- Why to get certified?
- How to plan and when will I complete the certifications if I start today?
- Is there any career track that I can follow to accomplish specialization level?

Furthermore, this guide provides a comprehensive career path towards being a specialist in the field of networking and also highlights the tracks needed to obtain certification.

IPS Personalized Technical Support for Customers: Good customer service means helping customers efficiently, in a friendly manner. It is essential to be able to handle issues for customers and do your best to ensure they are satisfied. Providing good service is one of the most important things that can set our business apart from the others of its kind.

Great customer service will result in attracting more customers and attain maximum customer retention.

IPS offers personalized TECH support to its customers to provide better value for money. If you have any queries related to technology and labs, you can simply ask our technical team for assistance via Live Chat or Email.

Our Products

Technology Workbooks

IPSpecialist Technology workbooks are the ideal guides to developing the hands-on skills necessary to pass the exam. Our workbooks cover the official exam blueprint and explain the technology with real life case study based labs. The content covered in each workbook consists of individually focused technology topics presented in an easy-to-follow, goal-oriented, step-by-step approach. Every scenario features detailed breakdowns and thorough verifications to help you completely understand the task and associated technology.

We extensively used mind maps in our workbooks to visually explain the technology. Our workbooks have become a widely used tool to learn and remember the information effectively.

vRacks

Our highly scalable and innovative virtualized lab platforms let you practice the IP Specialist Technology Workbook at your own time and your own place as per your convenience.

Quick Reference Sheets

Our quick reference sheets are a concise bundling of condensed notes of the complete exam blueprint. It is an ideal and handy document to help you remember the most important technology concepts related to the certification exam.

Practice Questions

IP Specialists' Practice Questions are dedicatedly designed from a certification exam perspective. The collection of these questions from our technology workbooks are prepared keeping the exam blueprint in mind covering not only important but necessary topics as well. It's an ideal document to practice and revise your certification.

Microsoft Certifications

Microsoft Azure Certifications are industry-recognized credentials that validate your technical Cloud skills and expertise while assisting you in your career growth. These are one of the most valuable IT certifications right now since Azure has established an overwhelming growth rate in the public cloud market. Even with the presence of several tough competitors such as Amazon Web Services, Google Cloud Engine, and Rackspace, Azure is going to be the dominant public cloud platform today, with an astounding collection of proprietary services that continues to grow.

In this certification, we will discuss cloud concepts where we will learn the core benefits of using Azure like high availability, scalability, etc. We will talk about the Azure Architecture in which cloud resources are put together to work at best; Azure Compute where you will learn how to run applications in Azure; Networking in which the discussion is on how Azure resources communicate with each other; Storage, where you put all of your data and have different ways of storing it. We will also be covering Databases that are used for storage of data, its efficient retrieval as per demand, and to make sure that the users have the right access to the resources. Also, we will counter some complex scenarios with their solutions. We will have discussions on important topics like; Security, which makes Azure the best secure choice for your applications and functions; Privacy, Compliance and Trust that make sure how services ensure privacy and how you stay compliant with standards; As well as, Pricing in Azure to stay ahead on cost.

AZ-900 is the first certification of Microsoft Azure, which is the foundational certificate in Azure. After this certification, you can prove to the world that you are proficient and have the credibility to reach the highest point of your professional life.

Value of Azure Certifications

Microsoft places equal emphasis on sound conceptual knowledge of its entire platform, as well as on hands-on experience with the Azure infrastructure and its many unique and complex components and services.

For Individuals

- Demonstrate your expertise in designing, deploying, and operating highly available, cost-effective, and secured applications on Microsoft Azure.
- Gain recognition and visibility of your proven skills and proficiency with Azure.
- Earn tangible benefits such as access to the Microsoft Certified Community, get invited to Microsoft Certification Appreciation Receptions and Lounges, obtain Microsoft

Certification Practice Exam Voucher and Digital Badge for certification validation, Microsoft Certified Logo usage.

- Foster credibility with your employer and peers.

For Employers

- Identify skilled professionals to lead IT initiatives with Cloud technologies.
- Reduce risks and costs to implement your workloads and projects on the Azure platform.
- Increase customer satisfaction.

Types of Certification

Role-based Certification

- Fundamental - Validates overall understanding of the Azure Cloud.
- Associate- Technical role-based certifications. No pre-requisite required.
- Expert- Highest level technical role-based certification.

About Microsoft Certified: Azure Fundamentals Exam

Exam Questions	Case study, short answer, repeated answer, MCQs
Number of Questions	40-60
Time to Complete	85 minutes
Exam Fee	99 USD

The Microsoft Certified: Azure Fundamentals exam validates cloud concepts, core Azure Services, Azure pricing and support, and the fundamentals of cloud security, privacy, compliance, and trust. Example concepts you should understand for this exam include:

- ➤ Cloud Concepts
- ➤ Core Azure Services
- ➤ Security, Privacy, Compliance, and Trust
- ➤ Azure Pricing and Support

Recommended Knowledge

- The benefits and considerations of using cloud services
- The differences between Infrastructure-as-a-Service (IaaS), Platform-as-a-Service (PaaS) and Software-as-a-Service (SaaS)
- The differences between public, private and hybrid cloud models
- The core Azure architectural components
- Core products and solutions available in Azure
- Azure management tools
- Securing network connectivity in Azure
- Azure identity services, security tools, and governance methodologies
- Monitoring and reporting in Azure
- Privacy, compliance, and data protection standards in Azure
- Azure subscriptions, planning and management tools
- Azure support options, SLAs, and service lifecycle

	Domain
Domain 1	Cloud Concepts
Domain 2	Core Azure Services
Domain 3	Security, Privacy, Compliance and Trust
Domain 4	Azure Pricing and Support

Practice Questions

1. An IT Engineer needs to create a Virtual Machine in Azure. Currently the IT Engineer has an Android OS based workstation. Which of the following can the IT Engineer use to create the desired Virtual Machine in Azure?

   A. Microsoft PowerApps
   B. Azure Cloud Shell
   C. Azure Powershell
   D. Azure CLI

Answer – B

Explanation:
On an Android OS, one can go to the Portal and launch Azure Cloud Shell as shown below

Option A is incorrect since PowerApps would not be used to create Virtual MachinesOptions C and D are incorrect since currently there is no clear stated definition on the support for Azure CLI or powershell support on Android OS.For more information on Azure Cloud Shell, please visit the belowURL https://azure.microsoft.com/en-us/features/cloud-shell/

2. Whom among the following can use the services offered as part of "Azure Germany"?
A. Only Enterprises in Germany
B. Only users located in Germany
C. Only Enterprises and users located in Germany
D. All customers who intend to do business in the EU

Answer - D

Explanation:
This is mentioned in the Microsoft documentation

Azure Germany is available to eligible customers and partners globally who intend to do business in the EU/EFTA, including the United Kingdom.

Since this is clearly mentioned, all other options are incorrect
For more information on Azure Germany, please visit the below URL
https://docs.microsoft.com/en-us/azure/germany/germany-welcome

3. A company is planning on setting up an Azure Free Account. Does the Standard Support plan come along with the Azure Free Account?
A. Yes
B. No

Answer – B

Explanation:

Basic support plan is the default one which is associated to all Azure accounts. In order to have Standard Support Plan, it needs to be purchased.

For more information on the comparison of Support plans, please visit the below URL

https://azure.microsoft.com/en-us/support/plans/

4. A company is planning on using their Azure Free Account for hosting production-based resources. Does the Azure Free Account allow you to host production-based resources?

A. Yes

B. No

Answer – A

Explanation:

Yes, you can, although you need to understand that you will need to pay for any extra charges that don't come under the Free Account conditions.

This is also mentioned in the Microsoft documentation

Can the Azure free account be used for production or only for development?

The Azure free account provides access to all Azure products and does not block customers from building their ideas into production. The Azure free account includes certain products—and specific quantities of those products—for free. To enable your production scenarios, you may need to use resources beyond the free amounts. You'll be billed for those additional resources at the pay-as-you-go service rates.

For more information on the Azure Free Account, please visit the below URL

https://azure.microsoft.com/en-us/free/free-account-faq/

5. Your company is planning on using Azure AD for authentication to the resources defined in Azure. Does Azure AD have built-in capabilities for securing authentication and authorization to resources?

A. Yes

B. No

Answer – A

Explanation:

For authentication, there are multiple ways to secure the sign in process. As shown in the Microsoft documentation below, you can use additional security options such as Security questions, Multi-Factor authentication etc.

Azure AD self-service password reset (SSPR) and Multi-Factor Authentication (MFA) may ask for additional information, known as authentication methods or security info, to confirm you are who you say you are when using the associated features.

Administrators can define in policy which authentication methods are available to users of SSPR and MFA. Some authentication methods may not be available to all features.

Microsoft highly recommends Administrators enable users to select more than the minimum required number of authentication methods in case they do not have access to one.

Authentication Method	Usage
Password	MFA and SSPR
Security questions	SSPR Only
Email address	SSPR Only
Microsoft Authenticator app	MFA and public preview for SSPR
OATH Hardware token	Public preview for MFA and SSPR
SMS	MFA and SSPR
Voice call	MFA and SSPR
App passwords	MFA only in certain cases

For authorization, you can use the various roles available in Azure. Below is the concept behind Role based access control in Azure

Role-based access control documentation

Role-based access control (RBAC) is a system that provides fine-grained access management of resources in Azure. Using RBAC, you can segregate duties within your team and grant only the amount of access to users that they need to perform their jobs.

For more information on Role based access control and authentication, please visit the below URL

https://docs.microsoft.com/en-us/azure/role-based-access-control/

https://docs.microsoft.com/en-us/azure/active-directory/authentication/concept-authentication-methods

6. A company is planning on purchasing Azure AD Basic for their Azure account. Does the Azure AD Basic tier come with an SLA of 99.9%?

A. Yes

B. No

Answer – A

Explanation:

Yes, this is also mentioned in the Microsoft documentation

SLA for Azure Active Directory

Last updated: June 2015

We guarantee at least 99.9% availability of the Azure Active Directory Basic and Premium services. The services are considered available in the following scenarios:

- Users are able to login to the service, login to the Access Panel, access applications on the Access Panel and reset passwords.

- IT administrators are able to create, read, write and delete entries in the directory or provision or de-provision users to applications in the directory.

No SLA is provided for the Free tier of Azure Active Directory.

For more information on Azure AD SLA, please visit the below URL

https://azure.microsoft.com/en-us/support/legal/sla/active-directory/v1_0/

7. A company is planning on upgrading their current Azure AD Free plan to the Azure AD Premium P1 plan. Does Microsoft provide the same feature set for both plans?

A. Yes

B. No

Answer – B

Explanation:

The support plans have different feature sets.

The Microsoft documentation mentions the following

	FREE	OFFICE 365 APPS	PREMIUM P1	PREMIUM P2
Core Identity and Access Management				
Directory Objects[1]	500,000 Object Limit	No Object Limit	No Object Limit	No Object Limit
Single Sign-On (SSO) [2]	up to 10 apps	up to 10 apps	unlimited	unlimited
User provisioning	✔	✔	✔	✔
Federated Authentication (ADFS or 3rd party IDP)	✔	✔	✔	✔
User and group management (add/update/delete)	✔	✔	✔	✔
Device registration	✔	✔	✔	✔

For more information on Azure Active Directory pricing details, please visit the following URL

- https://azure.microsoft.com/en-us/pricing/details/active-directory

8. A company wants to try out some services which are being offered by Azure in Public Preview. Do the services in Public Preview in Azure come with an SLA?

A. Yes
B. No

Answer – B

Explanation:

This is mentioned in the Microsoft documentation

Azure may include preview, beta, or other pre-release features, services, software, or regions offered by Microsoft to obtain customer feedback ("Previews"). Previews are made available to you on the condition that you agree to these terms of use, which supplement your agreement governing use of Azure.

PREVIEWS ARE PROVIDED "AS-IS," "WITH ALL FAULTS," AND "AS AVAILABLE," AND ARE EXCLUDED FROM THE SERVICE LEVEL AGREEMENTS AND LIMITED WARRANTY. Previews may not be covered by customer support. Previews may be subject to reduced or different security, compliance and privacy commitments, as further explained in the Microsoft Online Services Privacy Statement, Microsoft Azure Trust Center, the Online Services Terms, and any additional notices provided with the Preview. Customers should not use Previews to process Personal Data or other data that is subject to heightened compliance requirements. Certain named Previews may also be subject to additional terms set forth below, if any. We may change or discontinue Previews at any time without notice. We also may choose not to release a Preview into "General Availability."

For more information on Azure services preview terms, please visit the below URL

https://azure.microsoft.com/en-us/support/legal/preview-supplemental-terms/

9. A company wants to try out some services which are being offered by Azure in preview. Does Microsoft provide a separate portal for Azure portal specific previews?

A. Yes

B. No

Answer – A

Explanation:

Refer link for preview feature of Azue portal

https://preview.portal.azure.com/#home

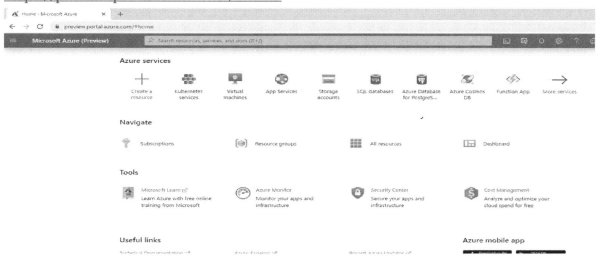

10. Your company needs to deploy and manage several Azure Web apps using the Azure App service resource. Which of the following URL would you use to manage the Azure Web Apps?

A. https://portal.microsoft.com

B. https://portal.azure.com

C. https://portal.azurewebsites.net

D. https://portal.azurewebsites.com

Answer – B

Explanation:

If you need to create and manage Azure Web apps, then you can do that from the Azure portal as shown below

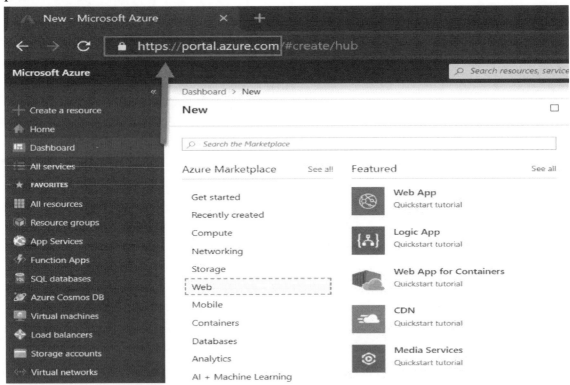

The URL for the Azure portal is https://portal.azure.com

For more information on the Azure portal, please visit the below URL

- https://azure.microsoft.com/en-us/features/azure-portal/

11. A company needs to store 2 TB worth of data that is infrequently used. The data needs to be accessed via Power BI. Which of the following could be used as a cost-effective data layer for this requirement?

A. Azure SQL databases

B. Azure PostgreSQL

C. Azure Cosmos DB

D. Azure Data Lake

Answer – D

Explanation:

And then you can replace the answer text with the following

If you are looking at storing data that is not frequently used, you can use the Azure Data Lake service.

The Microsoft documentation mentions the following

Connect Azure Data Lake Storage Gen2 for dataflow storage

12/16/2019 • 9 minutes to read • 🔵 🔵 🔵 🔵 🔵 +5

You can configure Power BI workspaces to store dataflows in your organization's Azure Data Lake Storage Gen2 account. This article describes the general steps necessary to do so, and provides guidance and best practices along the way. There are some advantages to configuring workspaces to store dataflow definitions and datafiles in your data lake, including the following:

- Azure Data Lake Storage Gen2 provides an enormously scalable storage facility for data
- Dataflow data and definition files can be leveraged by your IT department's developers to leverage Azure Data and artificial intelligence (AI) services as demonstrated in the GitHub samples from Azure Data Services
- Enables developers in your organization to integrate dataflow data into internal applications, and line-of-business solutions, using developer resources for dataflows and Azure

You should use Azure SQL, Azure PostgreSQL or Cosmos DB for frequently accessed data.

For more information on using Power BI with Azure Data Lake Storage, please visit the following URL

- https://docs.microsoft.com/en-us/power-bi/service-dataflows-connect-azure-data-lake-storage-gen2

12. A company wants to ensure that users in their company are authenticated when they access resources defined in their Azure account. Which of the following is the correct definition of authentication?

   A. This specifies the type of service you can use in Azure
   B. This specifies the type of data you can use in Azure
   C. This is the act of providing legitimate credentials
   D. This specifies what you can do in Azure

Answer – C

Explanation:

The definition of Authentication and Authorization is given in the Microsoft documentation

What is authentication?

09/24/2018 • 6 minutes to read • Contributors 🌑 🌑 🌑

Authentication is the act of challenging a party for legitimate credentials, providing the basis for creation of a security principal to be used for identity and access control. In simpler terms, it's the process of proving you are who you say you are. Authentication is sometimes shortened to AuthN.

Authorization is the act of granting an authenticated security principal permission to do something. It specifies what data you're allowed to access and what you can do with it. Authorization is sometimes shortened to AuthZ.

The other options are all incorrect because these are all user cases of Authorization
For more information on authentication, please visit the below URL
https://docs.microsoft.com/en-us/azure/active-directory/develop/authentication-scenarios

13. A company is planning on creating several Virtual Machines in Azure. Which of the following is the right category to which the Azure Virtual Machine belongs to?

A. Infrastructure as a service (IaaS)

B. Platform as a service (PaaS)

C. Software as a service (SaaS)

D. Function as a service (FaaS)

Answer – A

Explanation:

The Microsoft documentation gives an example of the difference between IaaS, PaaS and SaaS as shown below

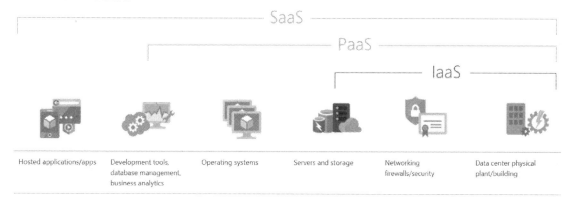

IaaS constitutes the Infrastructure which constitutes your Azure Virtual Machines.

Since this is clearly shown, all other options are incorrect

For more information on what is IaaS, please visit the below URL

https://azure.microsoft.com/en-us/overview/what-is-iaas/

14. An IT Engineer needs to use Azure Cloud Shell. Which of the following icons would you use for this purpose?

A. Option 1

B. Option 2

C. Option 3

D. Option 4

Answer – A

Explanation:

You would use the shown symbol below to access Azure Cloud Shell

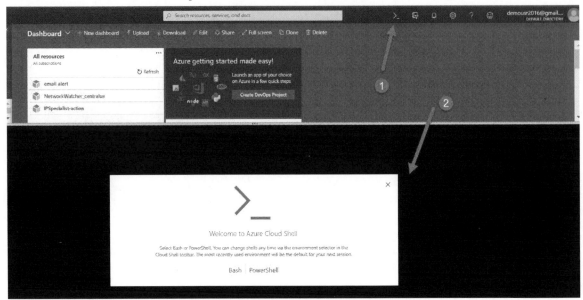

Since this is clearly shown, all other options are incorrect

For more information on Azure Cloud shell, please visit the below URL

https://azure.microsoft.com/en-us/features/cloud-shell/

Opion B is INCORRECT because this option is for "Notifications"

Option C is INCORRECT because this option is for "Settings"

Option D is INCORRECT because this option is for "Feedback"

15. A company needs to create around 50 customized Virtual Machines. Out of these 20 are Windows based Virtual machines and 30 are Ubuntu Machines. Which of the following would help reduce the administrative effort required to deploy the machines?

A. Azure Load Balancer

B. Azure Web Apps

C. Azure Traffic Manager

D. Azure ScaleSets

Answer – D

Explanation:

The Microsoft documentation mentions the following

- **Easy to create and manage multiple VMs**
  - When you have many VMs that run your application, it's important to maintain a consistent configuration across your environment. For reliable performance of your application, the VM size, disk configuration, and application installs should match across all VMs.
  - With scale sets, all VM instances are created from the same base OS image and configuration. This approach lets you easily manage hundreds of VMs without additional configuration tasks or network management.
  - Scale sets support the use of the Azure load balancer for basic layer-4 traffic distribution, and Azure Application Gateway for more advanced layer-7 traffic distribution and SSL termination.

Option A is incorrect since this is used to divert traffic to back end virtual machines at the network layer

Option B is incorrect since is used to host web applications

Option C is incorrect since this is used for DNS based traffic routing

For more information on Virtual Machine Scale sets, please visit the below URL

https://docs.microsoft.com/en-us/azure/virtual-machine-scale-sets/overview

16. A company wants to make use of Azure for deployment of various solutions. They want to ensure that whenever users authenticate to Azure, they have to make use of Multi-Factor Authentication. Which of the following can help them achieve this?

A. Azure Service Trust Portal

B. Azure Security Centre

C. Azure DDoS protection

D. Azure privileged identity management

Answer – D

Explanation:

With Azure Privileged Identity Management, you can make use of Multi-factor authentication (MFA) to activate any role for users. The Microsoft documentation mentions the following

What does it do?

Privileged Identity Management provides time-based and approval-based role activation to mitigate the risks of excessive, unnecessary, or misused access permissions on resources that you care about. Here are some of the key features of Privileged Identity Management:

- Provide **just-in-time** privileged access to Azure AD and Azure resources
- Assign **time-bound** access to resources using start and end dates
- Require **approval** to activate privileged roles
- Enforce **multi-factor authentication** to activate any role
- Use **justification** to understand why users activate
- Get **notifications** when privileged roles are activated
- Conduct **access reviews** to ensure users still need roles
- Download **audit history** for internal or external audit

Option A is incorrect since Service Trust Portal provide information about Microsoft Cloud services compliance with data protection standards and regulatory requirements, such as: International Organization for Standardization (ISO) Service Organization Controls (SOC) National Institute of Standards and Technology (NIST)

Option B is incorrect since this is a unified infrastructure security management system in Azure

Option C is incorrect since this is a solely a solution to protect against DDoS attacks

For more information on how to use MFA policies in Azure Privileged Identity Management, please visit the below URL

https://docs.microsoft.com/en-us/azure/active-directory/privileged-identity-management/pim-configure

17. A company is planning on hosting 2 Virtual Machines in Azure as shown below

Virtual Machine Name	Virtual Machine Size
demovm	B1S
demovm1	B1S

When the virtual machine demovm is stopped, will you still incur costs for the storage attached to the Virtual Machine?

A. Yes

B. No

Answer – A

Explanation:

The Disks attached to a Virtual Machine have different costs associated with them.

Below is a screenshot from the pricing calculator for a Virtual Machine. You can see that there is a dependency on the OS Disk.

For more information on the pricing calculator, please visit the below URL

https://azure.microsoft.com/en-us/pricing/calculator/

18. Which of the following is true when it comes to SaaS (Software as a service)?

A. You are responsible for scalability of the solution

B. You are responsible for the maintenance of the underlying hardware

C. You are responsible for configuring the solution

D. You are responsible for high availability of the solution

Answer – C

Explanation:

Below is a snapshot from the Microsoft documentation on SaaS solutions

Advantages of SaaS

Gain access to sophisticated applications. To provide SaaS apps to users, you don't need to purchase, install, update, or maintain any hardware, middleware, or software. SaaS makes even sophisticated enterprise applications, such as ERP and CRM, affordable for organizations that lack the resources to buy, deploy, and manage the required infrastructure and software themselves.

Pay only for what you use. You also save money because the SaaS service automatically scales up and down according to the level of usage.

Use free client software. Users can run most SaaS apps directly from their web browser without needing to download and install any software, although some apps require plugins. This means that you don't need to purchase and install special software for your users.

Mobilize your workforce easily. SaaS makes it easy to "mobilize" your workforce because users can access SaaS apps and data from any Internet-connected computer or mobile device. You don't need to worry about developing apps to run on different types of computers and devices because the service provider has already done so. In addition, you don't need to bring special expertise onboard to manage the security issues inherent in mobile computing. A carefully chosen service provider will ensure the security of your data, regardless of the type of device consuming it.

Access app data from anywhere. With data stored in the cloud, users can access their information from any Internet-connected computer or mobile device. And when app data is stored in the cloud, no data is lost if a user's computer or device fails.

Here you don't need to worry about the solution itself, the scalability or availability. You just managed the configuration.

Hence all of the other options are incorrect based on the concept of a SaaS solution.

For more information on SaaS, please visit the below URL

https://azure.microsoft.com/en-us/overview/what-is-saas/

19. A company is planning on setting up an Enterprise Azure Subscription. Do they need to have a valid Microsoft account for associating the Azure Subscription?

A. Yes

B. No

Answer – A

Explanation:

When you sign into an Azure account, you need to sign in with a valid Microsoft account as shown below

This could be a Work, School or Personal account. The Enterprise Agreement subscription just provides a means on how resources get billed for the subscription.

One can contact Microsoft for the Enterprise Agreement via the following URL

https://azure.microsoft.com/en-us/pricing/purchase-options/enterprise-agreement/

20. An IT administrator for a company has been given a powershell script. This powershell script will be used to create several Virtual Machines in Azure. You have to provide a machine to the IT administrator for running the powershell script.You decide to provide a Linux machine which has the Azure CLI tools installed.Would this solution fit the requirement?

A. Yes
B. No

Answer – B

Explanation:

We can execute Powershell scripts on Linux only when Powershell Core and Azure CLI is installed.

https://docs.microsoft.com/en-us/azure/devops/pipelines/tasks/deploy/azure-cli?view=azure-devops

https://docs.microsoft.com/en-us/azure/virtual-machines/linux/run-command

21. An IT administrator for a company has been given a powershell script. This powershell script will be used to create several Virtual Machines in Azure. You have to provide a machine to the IT administrator for running the powershell script.You decide to provide a ChromeOS based machine and use Azure Cloud Shell. Would this solution fit the requirement?

A. Yes
B. No

Answer – A

Explanation:

From the Azure Portal, if you use Azure Cloud Shell, you can run both Bash and powershell based scripts

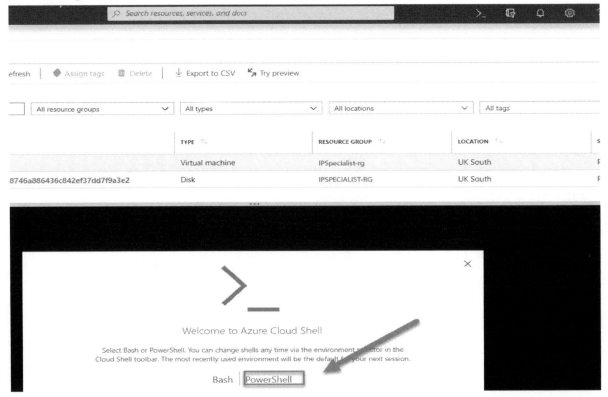

For more information on Azure CloudShell, please visit the below URL

- https://azure.microsoft.com/en-us/features/cloud-shell/
- https://docs.microsoft.com/en-us/azure/cloud-shell/overview
- https://docs.microsoft.com/en-us/azure/cloud-shell/persisting-shell-storage

22. An IT administrator for a company has been given a powershell script. This powershell script will be used to create several Virtual Machines in Azure. You have to provide a machine to the IT administrator for running the powershell script.You decide to provide a computer that has MacOS and Powershell Core 6.0 installed.Would this solution fit the requirement?

A. Yes
B. No

Answer – A

Explanation:

Yes, you can install Powershell on MacOS and then run the powershell scripts

For more information on installing powershell on MacOS, please visit the below URL

https://docs.microsoft.com/en-us/powershell/scripting/install/installing-powershell-core-on-macos?view=powershell-6

23. A company is planning on setting up a solution in Azure. The solution would have the following key requirement

- An Integration solution for the deployment of code

Which of the following would be best suited for this requirement?

A. Azure Advisor
B. Azure Cognitive Services
C. Azure Application Insights
D. Azure Devops

Answer – D

Explanation:

Azure Devops consists of a large set of tools. Amongst these you have Azure Pipelines which can be used to build, test and deploy code.

Azure Boards

Deliver value to your users faster using proven agile tools to plan, track, and discuss work across your teams.

Learn more >

Azure Pipelines

Build, test, and deploy with CI/CD that works with any language, platform, and cloud. Connect to GitHub or any other Git provider and deploy continuously.

Learn more >

Azure Repos

Get unlimited, cloud-hosted private Git repos and collaborate to build better code with pull requests and advanced file management.

Learn more >

Azure Test Plans

Test and ship with confidence using manual and exploratory testing tools.

Learn more >

Azure Artifacts

Create, host, and share packages with your team, and add artifacts to your CI/CD pipelines with a single click.

Learn more >

Extensions Marketplace

Access extensions from Slack to SonarCloud to 1,000 other apps and services—built by the community.

Learn more >

Since this is a clear feature on the tool, all other options are incorrect

For more information on Azure Devops, please visit the below URL

https://azure.microsoft.com/en-us/services/devops/

24. A company is planning on setting up a solution in Azure. The solution would have the following key requirement

- A tool that provides guidance and recommendations to improve an Azure environment

Which of the following would be best suited for this requirement?

A. Azure Advisor

B. Azure Cognitive Services

C. Azure Application Insights

D. Azure Devops

Answer – A

Explanation:

This is clearly mentioned in the Microsoft documentation

What is Advisor?

Advisor is a personalized cloud consultant that helps you follow best practices to optimize your Azure deployments. It analyzes your resource configuration and usage telemetry and then recommends solutions that can help you improve the cost effectiveness, performance, high availability, and security of your Azure resources.

With Advisor, you can:

- Get proactive, actionable, and personalized best practices recommendations.
- Improve the performance, security, and high availability of your resources, as you identify opportunities to reduce your overall Azure spend.
- Get recommendations with proposed actions inline.

Since this is a clear feature on the tool, all other options are incorrect

For more information on Azure Advisor, please visit the below URL

https://docs.microsoft.com/en-us/azure/advisor/advisor-overview

25. A company is planning on setting up a solution in Azure. The solution would have the following key requirement
- A simplified tool to build intelligent Artificial Intelligence applications

Which of the following would be best suited for this requirement?

    A. Azure Advisor

    B. Azure Cognitive Services

    C. Azure Application Insights

    D. Azure Devops

Answer – B

Explanation:

As shown in the Microsoft documentation below, the Azure Cognitive services has an entire list of features that can be used to build Artificial Intelligent based applications.

Use AI to solve business problems

Vision
Image-processing algorithms to smartly identify, caption, index, and moderate your pictures and videos.

Speech
Convert spoken audio into text, use voice for verification, or add speaker recognition to your app.

Knowledge
Map complex information and data in order to solve tasks such as intelligent recommendations and semantic search.

Search
Add Bing Search APIs to your apps and harness the ability to comb billions of webpages, images, videos, and news with a single API call.

Language
Allow your apps to process natural language with pre-built scripts, evaluate sentiment and learn how to recognize what users want.

Since this is a clear feature on the tool, all other options are incorrect

For more information on Azure Cognitive services, please visit the below URL

https://azure.microsoft.com/en-us/services/cognitive-services/

26. A company is planning on setting up a solution in Azure. The solution would have the following key requirement

- A tool used to monitor Web applications hosted in production based environments

Which of the following would be best suited for this requirement?

A. Azure Advisor

B. Azure Cognitive Services

C. Azure Application Insights

D. Azure Devops

Answer – C

Explanation:

This is clearly mentioned in the Microsoft documentation

What is Application Insights?

01/23/2019 · 5 minutes to read · Contributors 🖼️ 🔵 🔵

Application Insights is an extensible Application Performance Management (APM) service for web developers on multiple platforms. Use it to monitor your live web application. It will automatically detect performance anomalies. It includes powerful analytics tools to help you diagnose issues and to understand what users actually do with your app. It's designed to help you continuously improve performance and usability. It works for apps on a wide variety of platforms including .NET, Node.js and J2EE, hosted on-premises, hybrid, or any public cloud. It integrates with your DevOps process, and has connection points to a variety of development tools. It can monitor and analyze telemetry from mobile apps by integrating with Visual Studio App Center.

Since this is a clear feature on the tool, all other options are incorrect

For more information on Azure Application Insights, please visit the below URL

https://docs.microsoft.com/en-us/azure/azure-monitor/app/app-insights-overview

27. A company needs to implement a solution in Azure. Below are the key requirements for this solution
- Ability to store JSON documents
- Ensure low latency access to data from around the world

Which of the following data solution would you consider for this requirement?

   A. Azure SQL Database
   B. Azure CosmosDB
   C. Azure SQL Datawarehouse
   D. SQL Server Stretch database

Answer – B

Explanation:

The Microsoft documentation mentions the following when it comes to the features of CosmosDB

Guaranteed low latency at 99th percentile, worldwide

Using Cosmos DB, you can build highly responsive, planet scale applications. With its novel multi-master replication protocol and latch-free and write-optimized database engine, Cosmos DB guarantees less than 10-ms latencies for both, reads and (indexed) writes at the 99th percentile, all around the world. This capability enables sustained ingestion of data and blazing-fast queries for highly responsive apps.

Embedding data

When you start modeling data in a document store, such as Azure Cosmos DB, try to treat your entities as **self-contained documents** represented in JSON.

Option A is incorrect since this is used to store normal table like data

Option C is incorrect since this is used for building data warehouses

Option D is incorrect since this is used to dynamically stretch warm and cold transactional data from Microsoft SQL Server 2016 to Microsoft Azure

For more information on Azure CosmosDB, please visit the below URL

https://docs.microsoft.com/en-us/azure/cosmos-db/introduction

28. A company is planning on deploying Azure resources to a resource group. But the resources would belong to different locations. Can you have resources that belong to the same resource group but be in multiple locations?

A. Yes

B. No

Answer – A

Explanation:

An example is shown below in Azure, where you can have resources in same resource groups, but different locations.

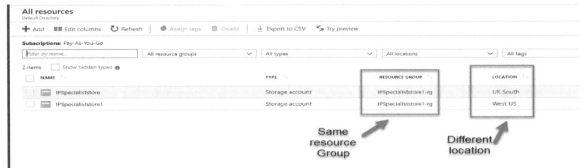

For more information on Azure Resource Manager, please visit the below URL

- https://docs.microsoft.com/en-us/azure/azure-resource-manager/resource-group-overview

29. A company is planning on deploying Azure resources to a resource group. The company is planning on assigning tags to the resource groups. Would the resources in the resource group also inherit the same tags?

A. Yes

B. No

Answer – B

Explanation:

An example is shown below where a resource group has a tag defined.

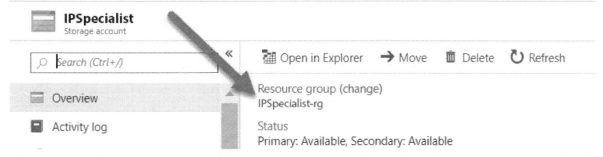

And there is a resource defined in the resource group

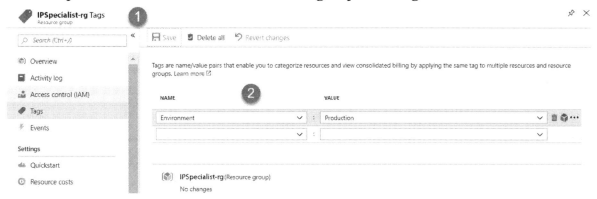

If you go to the Tags section of the resource, you will see that there are no tags defined

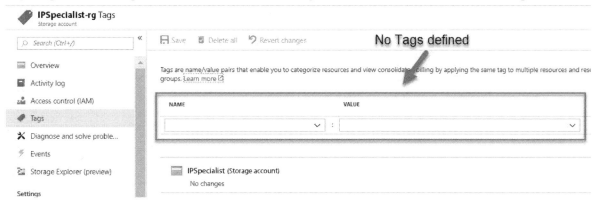

For more information on Azure Resource Group Tags, please visit the below URL

30. A company is planning on deploying Azure resources to a resource group. The company is planning on assigning permissions to the resource groups. Would the resources in the resource group also inherit the same permissions?

A. Yes

B. No

Answer – A

Explanation:

An example is shown below where a resource group has a permission defined.

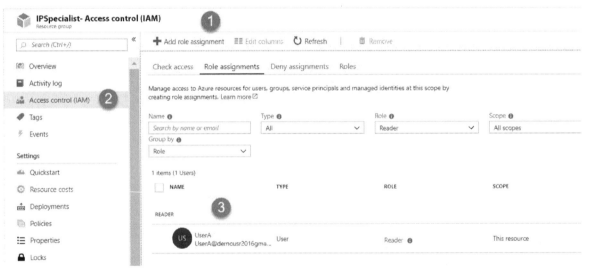

And there is a resource defined in the resource group

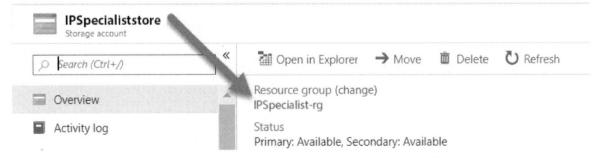

If you go to the Access Control section of the resource, you will see that the permissions are inherited from the resource group.

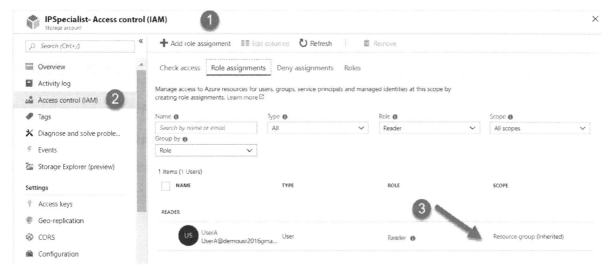

For more information on role-based access control, please visit the below URL

https://docs.microsoft.com/en-us/azure/role-based-access-control/role-assignments-portal

31. A company has a set of resources deployed to Azure. They want to make use of the Azure Advisor tool. Would the Azure Advisor tool alone be able to give recommendations on how to improve the security of the Azure AD environment?

A. Yes
B. No

Answer – B

Explanation:

The below screenshot from Azure documentation shows what Azure Advisor does. Azure Advisor integrates with Azure Security Center to give security recommendations to Azure AD (also to all the Azure Resources)

Make resources more secure with Azure Advisor

01/29/2019 · 2 minutes to read · Contributors 👤👤👤👤👤 all

Azure Advisor provides you with a consistent, consolidated view of recommendations for all your Azure resources. It integrates with Azure Security Center to bring you security recommendations. You can get security recommendations from the **Security** tab on the Advisor dashboard.

Security Center helps you prevent, detect, and respond to threats with increased visibility into and control over the security of your Azure resources. It periodically analyzes the security state of your Azure resources. When Security Center identifies potential security vulnerabilities, it creates recommendations. The recommendations guide you through the process of configuring the controls you need.

Azure Security can give you recommendations on how to secure your resources in Azure. Azure AD is already a secure platform. You should instead focus on how to secure sign-ins that occur using Azure AD.

For more information on Azure AD security recommendations, please visit the below URL

https://docs.microsoft.com/en-us/azure/advisor/advisor-security-recommendations

32. A company has a requirement to deploy 10 Azure resources for several departments. All of the resource types and configurations are the same. Which of the following could be used to automate the deployment of the resources using infrastructure as code?

A. Azure Resource Manager templates

B. Virtual machine scale sets

C. Azure API Management service

D. Management groups

Answer – A

Explanation:

The Microsoft documentation gives the definition of a template as shown below

• **Resource Manager template** - A JavaScript Object Notation (JSON) file that defines one or more resources to deploy to a resource group or subscription. The template can be used to deploy the resources consistently and repeatedly. See Template deployment.

Resource Manager templates are the ideal solution when you have to deploy the same type of resource repeatedly

Option B is incorrect since this is good only if you need to automate the deployment of Virtual Machines

Option C is incorrect since this is used for making API calls to Azure

Option D is incorrect since this is used to group your resources within subscriptions

For more information on Resource Manager, please visit the below URL

https://docs.microsoft.com/en-us/azure/azure-resource-manager/resource-group-overview

33. A company is planning on hosting solutions on the Azure Cloud. They need to implement MFA for identities hosted in Azure. Is it necessary to deploy a federation solution or sync on-premise identities to the cloud?

A. Yes

B. No

Answer – B

Explanation:

There are various ways to implement MFA on Azure, like using Conditional Access policies. In Azure AD, you can also manage MFA settings as shown below

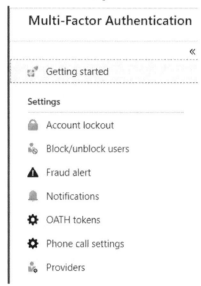

For more information on how to configure MFA settings, please visit the below URL

https://docs.microsoft.com/en-us/azure/active-directory/authentication/howto-mfa-mfasettings

34. A company has deployed their solutions on to Azure. They have users that connect to Azure AD via the Internet. They have the requirement that if users try to login from an anonymous IP address, they are then prompted to change their password. Which of the following should the company consider for this requirement?

A. Azure AD Connect Health

B. Azure AD Privileged Identity Management

C. Azure Advanced Threat Protection (ATP)

D. Azure AD Identity Protection

Answer – D

Explanation:

You have to create a policy in Azure AD Identity Protection. An example is shown below

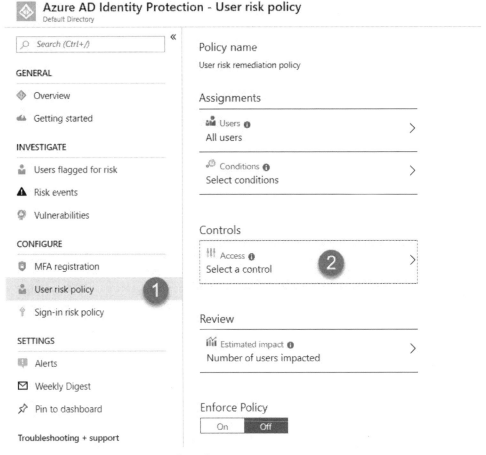

1. First go to User risk policy
2. Next go to Controls

Then based on the user sign in risk condition, you can make the user change the password as per the policy

Option A is incorrect since this is used to check the health status of Azure AD Connect

Option B is incorrect since is used for privileged level access in Azure

Option C is incorrect since this is used to protect resources in Azure

For more information on Azure AD Identity protection, please visit the below URL

https://docs.microsoft.com/en-us/azure/active-directory/identity-protection/overview

35. A company plans to setup multiple resources in their Azure subscription. They want to implement tagging of resources in Azure. But they want to ensure that when resource groups are created, they have to contain a tag with a name of "organization" and value of "ipspecialist".

You recommend using Azure locks for implementing this requirement

A. Yes
B. No

Answer – B

Explanation:

Azure locks are used to prevent accidental modification or deletion of resources in Azure.

For more information on Azure locks, please visit the below URL

https://docs.microsoft.com/en-us/azure/azure-resource-manager/resource-group-lock-resources

36. A company plans to setup multiple resources in their Azure subscription. They want to implement tagging of resources in Azure. But they want to ensure that when resource groups are created, they have to contain a tag with a name of "organization" and value of "ipspecialist".

You recommend using Azure policies for implementing this requirement

Would this recommendation fulfil the requirement?

A. Yes
B. No

Answer – A

Explanation:

Yes, you can use Azure policies. For this, there is also an inbuilt policy that can be used as shown below to implement tagging for resources groups

For more information on Azure policies, please visit the below URL

https://docs.microsoft.com/en-us/azure/governance/policy/overview

37. A company plans to setup multiple resources in their Azure subscription. They want to implement tagging of resources in Azure. But they want to ensure that when resource groups are created, they have to contain a tag with a name of "organization" and value of "ipspecialist".

You recommend using Azure Key Vault for implementing this requirement

Would this recommendation fulfil the requirement?

A. Yes
B. No

Answer – B

Explanation:

Azure Key vault is used for security purposes such as key and secret management

For more information on Azure key vault, please visit the below URL

https://docs.microsoft.com/en-us/azure/key-vault/key-vault-whatis

38. A company has created a resource group as shown below. They want to ensure that resources within the resource group don't get accidentally deleted.

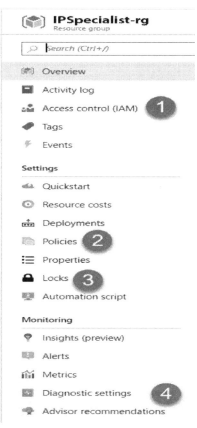

Which of the following would you use for this purpose?

A. Access Control

B. Policies

C. Locks

D. Diagnostics settings

Answer – C

Explanation:

The Microsoft documentation mentions the following

Lock resources to prevent unexpected changes

11/08/2018 · 5 minutes to read · Contributors 🟢 🔵 🟠 🔴 ⚫ all

As an administrator, you may need to lock a subscription, resource group, or resource to prevent other users in your organization from accidentally deleting or modifying critical resources. You can set the lock level to **CanNotDelete** or **ReadOnly**. In the portal, the locks are called **Delete** and **Read-only** respectively.

- **CanNotDelete** means authorized users can still read and modify a resource, but they can't delete the resource.
- **ReadOnly** means authorized users can read a resource, but they can't delete or update the resource. Applying this lock is similar to restricting all authorized users to the permissions granted by the **Reader** role.

Option A is incorrect since this is used to set the permission for resources

Option B is incorrect since this is used for governance purposes

Option D is incorrect since this is used enable diagnostics on the underlying resource

For more information on Azure locks, please visit the below URL

https://docs.microsoft.com/en-us/azure/azure-resource-manager/resource-group-lock-resources

39. A company wants to purchase an Azure support plan. Below is a key requirement from the support plan

- Regular architecture reviews from Microsoft for the company's Azure environment

Which of the following plan would the company need to purchase to fulfil this requirement?

    A. Premier

    B. Developer

    C. Professional Direct

    D. Standard

Answer – A

Explanation:

From the Support plans as shown below, you can see that only the Premier plan has the required architecture support

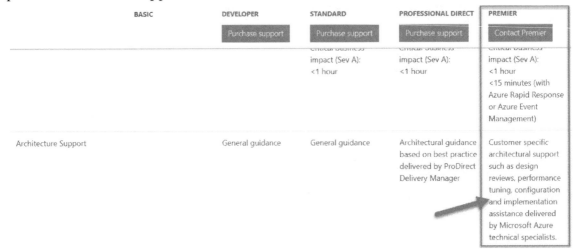

	BASIC	DEVELOPER	STANDARD	PROFESSIONAL DIRECT	PREMIER
		Purchase support	Purchase support	Purchase support	Contact Premier
			impact (Sev A): <1 hour	impact (Sev A): <1 hour	impact (Sev A): <1 hour <15 minutes (with Azure Rapid Response or Azure Event Management)
Architecture Support		General guidance	General guidance	Architectural guidance based on best practice delivered by ProDirect Delivery Manager	Customer specific architectural support such as design reviews, performance tuning, configuration and implementation assistance delivered by Microsoft Azure technical specialists.

Since this is clear from the documentation, all other options are incorrect

For more information on the support plans, please visit the below URL

https://azure.microsoft.com/en-us/support/plans/

40. A company has a set of Virtual machines defined in Azure. One of the machines was down due to issues with the underlying Azure Infrastructure. The server was down for an extended period of time and breached the standard SLA defined by Microsoft. How will Microsoft reimburse the downtime cost?

    A. By directly sending money to the customer's bank account
    B. By spinning up another Virtual Machine free of cost for the client
    C. By providing service credits to the customer
    D. By providing a service free of cost to use for a specific duration of time.

Answer – C

Explanation:

If you look at the pricing FAQ, you can see that Microsoft offers Service level credits if it does not meet the SLA targets

What are the Azure SLA Credits?

Azure SLA Credits are calculated on a per subscription basis as a percentage of the bill for that service in the billing month that the SLA was missed. The service credits are applied to the subsequent month's bill. Generally, we provide 10% credit if we fall below the first threshold (99.95% or 99.9%, depending on the service) and 25% if we fall beneath the subsequent threshold (99%). Please refer to our SLA page for complete details.

Since this is clearly given in the documentation, all other options are incorrect

For more information on Azure pricing FAQ's, please visit the below URL

https://azure.microsoft.com/en-us/pricing/faq/

41. A company is planning on moving to Azure. The senior management wants to get an idea on the cost that would be incurred when hosting resources in Azure.

You recommend using the Azure Cost Management to get the required costing of the resources

Would this recommendation fit the requirement?

    A. Yes
    B. No

Answer – B

Explanation:

The Cost Management feature is great to give you a breakdown of the cost once the resources are hosted in Azure. It will not give you an indication of costs that can be incurred when using Azure. Below is a snapshot of Cost Management in Azure

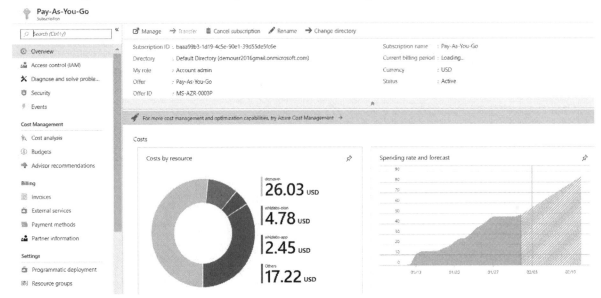

For more information on Azure Cost Management, please visit the below URL

https://azure.microsoft.com/en-us/pricing/details/cost-management/

42. A company is planning on moving to Azure. The senior management wants to get an idea on the cost that would be incurred when hosting resources in Azure.

You recommend using the Cloudyn service to get the required costing of the resources Would this recommendation fit the requirement?

A. Yes

B. No

Answer – B

Explanation:

The Microsoft documentation mentions the below details on the Cloudyn service. It will not give you an indication of costs that can be incurred when using Azure

What is the Cloudyn service?

12/06/2018 · 2 minutes to read · Contributors

Cloudyn, a Microsoft subsidiary, allows you to track cloud usage and expenditures for your Azure resources and other cloud providers including AWS and Google. Easy-to-understand dashboard reports help with cost allocation and showbacks/chargebacks as well. Cloudyn helps optimize your cloud spending by identifying underutilized resources that you can then manage and adjust.

For more information on the Cloudyn service, please visit the below URL

https://docs.microsoft.com/en-us/azure/cost-management/overview

43. A company is planning on moving to Azure. The senior management wants to get an idea on the cost that would be incurred when hosting resources in Azure.

You recommend using the pricing calculator to get the required costing of the resources

Would this recommendation fit the requirement?

A. Yes

B. No

Answer – A

Explanation:

The pricing calculator is the perfect tool for estimating the price of hosting resources in Azure

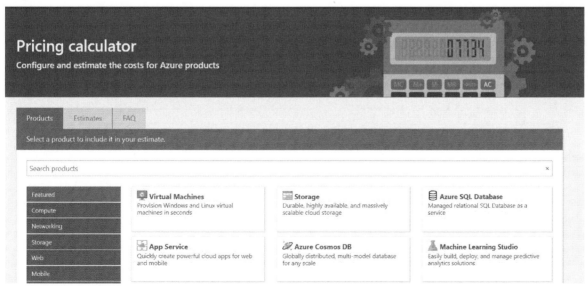

For more information on the Azure pricing calculator, please visit the below URL

https://azure.microsoft.com/en-us/pricing/calculator/

44. A company wants to host a mission critical application on a set of Virtual Machines in Azure. They want to ensure they can setup the infrastructure in Azure to guarantee the maximum possible uptime for the application. Which of the following can you make use of in Azure to fulfil this requirement? Choose 2 answers from the options given below

A. Resource Groups
B. Availability Zones
C. Availability Sets
D. Resource Tags

Answer – B and C

Explanation:

The Microsoft documentation mentions the following

Achieve High Availability faster in the cloud

As soon as you sign up, access the tools, the infrastructure, and the guidance you need to deploy your applications in the cloud. Support your most demanding mission-critical applications to build always-available sites cost-effectively. And take advantage of an SLA of up to 99.99 percent for your virtual machines.

High-availability solutions

Availability Zones >

Availability sets >

Virtual Machine Scale Sets (VMSS) >

Option A is incorrect since this is used to categorize resources

Option D is incorrect since this is used to improve categorization and billing of resources in Azure

For more information on resiliency in Azure, please visit the below URL

https://azure.microsoft.com/en-us/features/resiliency/

45. A company is planning on hosting an application on a set of Virtual Machines in Azure. They want to ensure that the application survives a region wide failure in

Azure. Which of the following concept needs to be considered to fulfil this requirement?

A. Scalability

B. Disaster Recovery

C. Agility

D. Elasticity

Answer – B

Explanation:

The Microsoft documentation mentions the following

Disaster recovery for Azure applications

09/12/2018 • 35 minutes to read • Contributors ● ● ● ● ● all

Disaster recovery (DR) is focused on recovering from a catastrophic loss of application functionality. For example, if an Azure region hosting your application becomes unavailable, you need a plan for running your application or accessing your data in another region.

Business and technology owners must determine how much functionality is required during a disaster. This level of functionality can take a few forms: completely unavailable, partially available via reduced functionality or delayed processing, or fully available.

Resiliency and high availability strategies are intended for handling temporary failure conditions. Executing this plan involves people, processes, and supporting applications that allow the system to continue functioning. Your plan should include rehearsing failures and testing the recovery of databases to ensure the plan is sound.

Option A is incorrect since this is used to scale in our scale out infrastructure

Option C is incorrect since this is used from a customer perspective to make applications more agile

Option D is incorrect since this is used to make an application more flexible in its architecture based on user demand

For more information on disaster recovery in Azure, please visit the below URL

https://docs.microsoft.com/en-us/azure/architecture/resiliency/disaster-recovery-azure-applications

46. A company is planning on implementing the below architecture

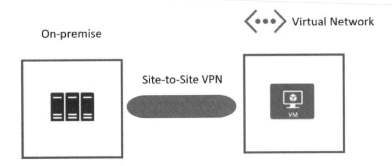

On-premise

Virtual Network

Site-to-Site VPN

Which of the following best describes the above cloud model?

A. Private Cloud

B. Public Cloud

C. Government Cloud

D. Hybrid Cloud

Answer – D

Explanation:

This is an example of having infrastructure hosted in both the Azure public cloud and in your on-premise network.

Option A is incorrect since there is an IaaS model specified on the right-hand side

Option B is incorrect since there is an on-premise server on the left-hand side

Option C is incorrect since there is no specification of a pure government cloud setup

For more information on some use cases for hybrid cloud scenarios is shown below, please visit the below URL

https://docs.microsoft.com/en-us/office365/enterprise/hybrid-cloud-scenarios-for-azure-iaas

47. A company wants to create multiple data stores in Azure. They want to have storage layers that can be used to store data that is infrequently used. Which of the following storage tiers for Azure BLOB storage would be suitable for this type of requirement? Choose 2 answers from the options given below

A. Premium storage

B. Hot storage

C. Cool storage

D. Archive storage

Answer – C and D

Explanation:

This is given in the Microsoft documentation

Azure Blob storage: Premium (preview), Hot, Cool, and Archive storage tiers

01/09/2018 · 17 minutes to read · Contributors ⬤ ⬤ ⬤ ⬤ ⬤ all

Overview

Azure storage offers different storage tiers, which allow you to store Blob object data in the most cost-effective manner. The available tiers include:

- **Premium storage (preview)** provides high-performance hardware for data that is accessed frequently.

- **Hot storage:** is optimized for storing data that is accessed frequently.

- **Cool storage** is optimized for storing data that is infrequently accessed and stored for at least 30 days.

- **Archive storage** is optimized for storing data that is rarely accessed and stored for at least 180 days with flexible latency requirements (on the order of hours).

Since this is provided in the Microsoft documentation, all other options are incorrect

For more information on blob storage tiers, please visit the below URL

https://docs.microsoft.com/en-us/azure/storage/blobs/storage-blob-storage-tiers

48. A company wants to have an Enterprise messaging solution integrated with their existing application hosted in Azure.

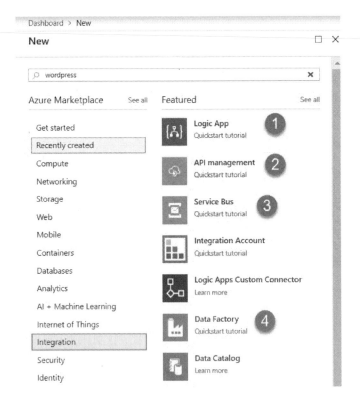

Which of the following would be the ideal service to use for this requirement?

A. Logic App

B. API management

C. Service Bus

D. Data Factory

Answer – C

Explanation:

The Microsoft documentation mentions the following on this service

What is Azure Service Bus?

09/22/2018 · 4 minutes to read · Contributors 👤👤👤👤 all

Microsoft Azure Service Bus is a fully managed enterprise integration message broker. Service Bus is most commonly used to decouple applications and services from each other, and is a reliable and secure platform for asynchronous data and state transfer. Data is transferred between different applications and services using *messages*. A message is in binary format, which can contain JSON, XML, or just text.

Some common messaging scenarios are:

- Messaging: transfer business data, such as sales or purchase orders, journals, or inventory movements.
- Decouple applications: improve reliability and scalability of applications and services (client and service do not have to be online at the same time).
- Topics and subscriptions: enable 1:*n* relationships between publishers and subscribers.
- Message sessions: implement workflows that require message ordering or message deferral.

Option A is incorrect since this is used as a workflow service

Option B is incorrect since this is used for managing API's

Option D is incorrect since this is used as an ETL service on the cloud

For more information on the Azure service Bus, please visit the below URL

https://docs.microsoft.com/en-us/azure/service-bus-messaging/service-bus-messaging-overview

49. A company is planning on hosting an application on a set of Virtual Machines. The Virtual Machines are going to be running for a pro-longed duration of time. Which of the following should be considered to reduce the overall cost of Virtual Machine usage?

A. Premium Disks

B. Virtual Machine Scale sets

C. Azure Reservations

D. Azure Resource Groups

Answer – C

Explanation:

The Microsoft documentation mentions the following

What are Azure Reservations?

08/08/2018 · 4 minutes to read · Contributors ●●●●● all

Azure Reservations helps you save money by pre-paying for one-year or three-years of virtual machine, SQL Database compute capacity, Azure Cosmos DB throughput, or other Azure resources. Pre-paying allows you to get a discount on the resources you use. Reservations can significantly reduce your virtual machine, SQL database compute, Azure Cosmos DB, or other resource costs up to 72% on pay-as-you-go prices. Reservations provide a billing discount and don't affect the runtime state of your resources.

Option A is incorrect since using Premium Disks is an expensive option

Option B is incorrect since this is used for scalability of your virtual machines

Option D is incorrect since this is used for grouping your Azure resources

For more information on Azure Cost Reservations, please visit the below URL

https://docs.microsoft.com/en-us/azure/billing/billing-save-compute-costs-reservations

50. A company has launched a set of Virtual Machines in their Pay-as-you-go Azure subscription. After launching a set of VM's they seem to be hitting a constraint of 20 vCPU's and are not able to provision additional Virtual Machines. Which of the following can be done to allow the company to provision more Virtual Machines?

A. Raise a support ticket with Microsoft

B. Increase the limit in the Azure portal

C. Increase the limit using the Azure CLI

D. Increase the limit in Azure Advisor

Answer – A

Explanation:

> ⓘ Note
>
> If you want to raise the limit or quota above the **Default Limit**, open an online customer support request at no charge. The limits can't be raised above the **Maximum Limit** value shown in the following tables. If there is no **Maximum Limit** column, then the resource doesn't have adjustable limits.
>
> Free Trial subscriptions are not eligible for limit or quota increases. If you have a Free Trial subscription, you can upgrade to a Pay-As-You-Go subscription. For more information, see Upgrade Azure Free Trial to Pay-As-You-Go and Free Trial subscription FAQ.

Since this is clearly mentioned in the Microsoft documentation, all other options are incorrect

For more information on Azure subscription service limits, please visit the below URL

https://docs.microsoft.com/en-us/azure/azure-subscription-service-limits

A company wants to set up users in their Azure Account. They have segregated their users into groups. They now want to ensure they set the right permissions for users and administrators accordingly. They need to manage the permissions effectively.

You recommend using Azure Policies

Does this recommendation meet the requirement?

    A. Yes

    B. No

Answer – B

Explanation:

Azure policies are used from more of a governance aspect. The Microsoft documentation mentions the following on Azure policies

What is Azure Policy?

12/06/2018 · 9 minutes to read · Contributors

Governance validates that your organization can achieve its goals through an effective and efficient use of IT. It meets this need by creating clarity between business goals and IT projects.

For more information on Azure policies, please visit the below URL

https://docs.microsoft.com/en-us/azure/governance/policy/overview

51. A company wants to setup users in their Azure Account. They have segregated their users into groups. They now want to ensure they set the right permissions for users and administrators accordingly. They need to manage the permissions effectively.

You recommend using Azure Role Based Access

Does this recommendation meet the requirement?

    A. Yes

    B. No

Answer – A

Explanation:

This is the right way to manage permissions. The Microsoft documentation mentions the following on Role Based Access control

What is role-based access control (RBAC)?

01/14/2019 • 7 minutes to read • Contributors ● ● ●

Access management for cloud resources is a critical function for any organization that is using the cloud. Role-based access control (RBAC) helps you manage who has access to Azure resources, what they can do with those resources, and what areas they have access to.

RBAC is an authorization system built on Azure Resource Manager that provides fine-grained access management of resources in Azure.

What can I do with RBAC?

Here are some examples of what you can do with RBAC:

- Allow one user to manage virtual machines in a subscription and another user to manage virtual networks
- Allow a DBA group to manage SQL databases in a subscription
- Allow a user to manage all resources in a resource group, such as virtual machines, websites, and subnets
- Allow an application to access all resources in a resource group

For more information on Role based access control, please visit the below URL

https://docs.microsoft.com/en-us/azure/role-based-access-control/overview

52. A company wants to setup users in their Azure Account. They have segregated their users into groups. They now want to ensure they set the right permissions for users and administrators accordingly. They need to manage the permissions effectively.

You recommend using Azure Management Groups

Does this recommendation meet the requirement?

    A. Yes

    B. No

Answer – B

Explanation:

Azure management groups are used for organizing resources in Azure. The Microsoft documentation mentions the following on Azure management groups.

Organize your resources with Azure management groups

02/19/2019 • 7 minutes to read • Contributors 🔵🔵🔵

If your organization has many subscriptions, you may need a way to efficiently manage access, policies, and compliance for those subscriptions. Azure management groups provide a level of scope above subscriptions. You organize subscriptions into containers called "management groups" and apply your governance conditions to the management groups. All subscriptions within a management group automatically inherit the conditions applied to the management group. Management groups give you enterprise-grade management at a large scale no matter what type of subscriptions you might have.

For example, you can apply policies to a management group that limits the regions available for virtual machine (VM) creation. This policy would be applied to all management groups, subscriptions, and resources under that management group by only allowing VMs to be created in that region.

Hierarchy of management groups and subscriptions

You can build a flexible structure of management groups and subscriptions to organize your resources into a hierarchy for unified policy and access management. The following diagram shows an example of creating a hierarchy for governance using management groups.

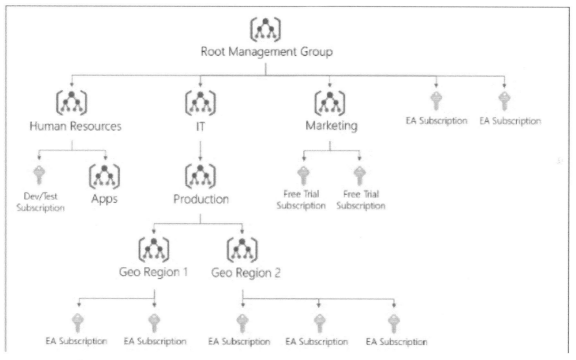

For more information on Azure Management Groups, please visit the below URL

https://docs.microsoft.com/en-us/azure/governance/management-groups/

53. A company wants to host their applications on Azure using serverless components. They don't want to manage the underlying infrastructure for the application.

Which of the following could be used to host code that could be run on a serverless infrastructure?

    A. Azure Logic Apps

    B. Azure Service Bus

    C. Azure Function

    D. Azure Storage

Answer – C

Explanation:

The Microsoft documentation mentions the following

An introduction to Azure Functions

10/03/2017 · 4 minutes to read · Contributors 👤 👤 👤 👤 👤 all

Azure Functions is a solution for easily running small pieces of code, or "functions," in the cloud. You can write just the code you need for the problem at hand, without worrying about a whole application or the infrastructure to run it. Functions can make development even more productive, and you can use your development language of choice, such as C#, F#, Node.js, Java, or PHP. Pay only for the time your code runs and trust Azure to scale as needed. Azure Functions lets you develop serverless applications on Microsoft Azure.

Option A is incorrect because this is designed to implement workflows in Azure

Option B is incorrect because this is used as a messaging service in Azure

Option D is incorrect because this is used as a storage service in Azure

For more information on Azure Functions, please visit the below URL

https://docs.microsoft.com/en-us/azure/azure-functions/functions-overview

54. A company wants to host their applications on Azure using serverless components. They don't want to manage the underlying infrastructure for the application.

Which of the following could be used to implement a workflow that could be run on a serverless infrastructure?

    A. Azure Logic Apps

    B. Azure Service Bus

    C. Azure Function App

    D. Azure Storage

Answer – A

Explanation:

The Microsoft documentation mentions the following

What is Azure Logic Apps?

06/29/2018 · 8 minutes to read · Contributors 🔵 🔵 ⚬

Azure Logic Apps is a cloud service that helps you automate and orchestrate tasks, business processes, and workflows when you need to integrate apps, data, systems, and services across enterprises or organizations. Logic Apps simplifies how you design and build scalable solutions for app integration, data integration, system integration, enterprise application integration (EAI), and business-to-business (B2B) communication, whether in the cloud, on premises, or both.

Option B is incorrect because this is used as a messaging service in Azure

Option C is incorrect because this is used to host functions in Azure

Option D is incorrect because this is used as a storage service in Azure

For more information on Azure Logic Apps, please visit the below URL

https://docs.microsoft.com/en-us/azure/logic-apps/logic-apps-overview

55. An IT Engineer needs to create a Virtual Machine in Azure. Currently the IT Engineer has a Windows desktop and has installed the Azure Command Line interface. Which of the following would the IT engineer need to install and then use the Azure Command Line Interface? Choose 2 answers from the options given below

A. Powershell

B. File and Print Explorer

C. Command Prompt

D. Control Panel

Answer – A and C

Explanation:

You can launch the Azure command line tool from command prompt as shown below

```
C:\Users\developer\AppData\Roaming\Python\Python36\Scripts>az login
To sign in, use a web browser to open the page https://microsoft.com/devicelogin and enter the code D887V
ZAN5 to authenticate.
```

Or you could also launch it from powershell as shown below

```
Windows PowerShell
Copyright (C) Microsoft Corporation. All rights reserved.

PS C:\Users\developer> az login
To sign in, use a web browser to open the page https://microsoft.com/devicelogin and enter the code DF4FUNACB
to authenticate.
```

Options B and D are incorrect because you can't launch Azure Command Line from any of these options.

For more information on Azure Command Line Interface, please visit the below URL

https://docs.microsoft.com/en-us/cli/azure/get-started-with-azure-cli?view=azure-cli-latest

56. A company is planning on setting up an Azure Free Account. Does the Standard Support plan come along with the Azure Free Account?

A. Yes

B. No

Answer – B

Explanation:

Basic support plan is the default one which is associated to all Azure accounts. In order to have Standard Support Plan, it needs to be purchased.

For more information on the comparison of Support plans, please visit the below URL

https://azure.microsoft.com/en-us/support/plans/

57. A customer is planning on creating several Azure Free Accounts. Can a customer have an allowance of a maximum of 10 Azure Free Accounts?

A. Yes

B. No

Answer – B

Explanation:

A customer can only have one Azure Free Account. This is also given in the Microsoft documentation

How many free account subscriptions am I allowed to sign up for?

There is a limit of one subscription with 12 months free access to products and $200 credit per new customer. You can, however, have multiple other subscription types (such as pay-as-you-go) within a single free account.

For more information on the Azure Free Account, please visit the below URL

58. Your company is planning on hosting resources in Azure. Is it possible for outside users to have access to resources in Azure?

    A. Yes
    B. No

Answer – A

Explanation:

Azure has other capabilities in place that can allow other users to access Azure-based resources. For example, Azure has the feature of Azure AD Business to Business collaboration where the users don't have to be defined in Azure.

The Microsoft documentation mentions the following on Azure B2B

Collaborate with any partner using their identities

With Azure AD B2B, the partner uses their own identity management solution, so there is no external administrative overhead for your organization.

- The partner uses their own identities and credentials; Azure AD is not required.
- You don't need to manage external accounts or passwords.
- You don't need to sync accounts or manage account lifecycles.

For more information on Azure B2B, please visit the below URL

https://docs.microsoft.com/en-us/azure/active-directory/b2b/what-is-b2b

59. A company is planning on purchasing Azure AD Premium for their Azure account. Does the Azure AD Premium tier come with an SLA of 99.9%?

    A. Yes
    B. No

Answer – A

Explanation:

Yes, this is also mentioned in the Microsoft documentation

SLA for Azure Active Directory

Last updated: June 2015

We guarantee at least 99.9% availability of the Azure Active Directory Basic and Premium services. The services are considered available in the following scenarios:

- Users are able to login to the service, login to the Access Panel, access applications on the Access Panel and reset passwords.
- IT administrators are able to create, read, write and delete entries in the directory or provision or de-provision users to applications in the directory.

No SLA is provided for the Free tier of Azure Active Directory.

For more information on Azure AD SLA, please visit the below URL

https://azure.microsoft.com/en-us/support/legal/sla/active-directory/v1_0/

60. A company wants to try out some services which are being offered by Azure in Public Preview. Should the company deploy resources which are part of Public Preview in their production environment?

    A. Yes

    B. No

Answer – B

Explanation:

As mentioned below in the Microsoft documentation, there is no SLA or guarantee for any service in Public Preview. So, you should not look at deploying such services in production

Supplemental Terms of Use for Microsoft Azure Previews

Last updated: December 2018

Azure may include preview, beta, or other pre-release features, services, software, or regions offered by Microsoft to obtain customer feedback ("Previews"). Previews are made available to you on the condition that you agree to these terms of use, which supplement your agreement governing use of Azure.

PREVIEWS ARE PROVIDED "AS-IS," "WITH ALL FAULTS," AND "AS AVAILABLE," AND ARE EXCLUDED FROM THE SERVICE LEVEL AGREEMENTS AND LIMITED WARRANTY. Previews may not be covered by customer support. Previews may be subject to reduced or different security, compliance and privacy commitments, as further explained in the Microsoft Online Services Privacy Statement, Microsoft Azure Trust Center, the Online Services Terms, and any additional notices provided with the Preview. Customers should not use Previews to process Personal Data or other data that is subject to heightened compliance requirements. Certain named Previews may also be subject to additional terms set forth below, if any. We may change or discontinue Previews at any time without notice. We also may choose not to release a Preview into "General Availability."

For more information on Azure services preview terms, please visit the below URL

https://azure.microsoft.com/en-us/support/legal/preview-supplemental-terms/

61. A company is planning on using Azure SQL Datawarehouse for hosting their sales historical data. Which of the following is a feature of the Azure SQL Datawarehouse architecture?

    A. High Availability

B. Scalability

C. Disaster Recovery

D. Visualization

Answer – B

Explanation:

The Microsoft documentation mentions the following on the scalability of the compute architecture of the Azure SQL Datawarehouse architecture

With decoupled storage and compute, SQL Data Warehouse can:

- Independently size compute power irrespective of your storage needs.
- Grow or shrink compute power without moving data.
- Pause compute capacity while leaving data intact, so you only pay for storage.
- Resume compute capacity during operational hours.

Options A and C are incorrect because this is something that you have to ensure with the capabilities available in Azure

Option D is incorrect since you need to use other tools for handling the visualization of data in a SQL Datawarehouse

For more information on the architecture for SQL Datawarehouse, please visit the below URL

https://docs.microsoft.com/en-us/azure/sql-data-warehouse/massively-parallel-processing-mpp-architecture

62. A company is planning on creating several SQL Databases in Azure. They would be using the Azure SQL Database service. Which of the following is the right category to which the Azure SQL Database service belongs to?

A. Infrastructure as a service (IaaS)

B. Platform as a service (PaaS)

C. Software as a service (SaaS)

D. Function as a service (FaaS)

Answer – B

Explanation:

This is given in the Microsoft documentation

- Azure SQL Database: A fully-managed SQL database engine, based on the latest stable Enterprise Edition of SQL Server. This is a relational database-as-a-service (DBaaS) hosted in the Azure cloud that falls into the industry category of *Platform-as-a-Service (PaaS)*. SQL database is built on standardized hardware and software that is owned, hosted, and maintained by Microsoft. With SQL Database, you can use built-in features and functionality that require extensive configuration in SQL Server. When using SQL Database, you pay-as-you-go with options to scale up or out for greater power with no interruption. SQL Database has additional features that are not available in SQL Server, such as built-in intelligence and management. Azure SQL Database offers several deployment options:

For more information on Azure SQL Databases, please visit the below URL

https://docs.microsoft.com/en-us/azure/sql-database/sql-database-paas-vs-sql-server-iaas

63. A company is planning on using Azure Storage Accounts. They have the following requirement
- Storage of 2 TB of data
- Storage of a million files

Would using Azure Storage fulfil these requirements?

A. Yes

B. No

Answer – A

Explanation:

If you look at the Microsoft documentation, Azure storage has a high limit on the amount that can be stored and no limit on the number of files

Standard storage account scale limits

The following table describes default limits for Azure Storage. The *ingress* limit refers to all data (requests) being sent to a storage account. The *egress* limit refers to all data (responses) being received from a storage account.

Resource	Default limit
Number of storage accounts per region per subscription, including both standard and premium accounts	250
Max storage account capacity	2 PB for US and Europe, 500 TB for all other regions including UK
Max number of blob containers, blobs, file shares, tables, queues, entities, or messages per storage account	No limit

For more information on Azure storage capabilities, please visit the below URL

https://docs.microsoft.com/en-us/azure/storage/common/storage-scalability-targets

64. A company is planning on using Azure Storage Accounts. They have the following requirement

- Replication of data to another region

Can the Azure storage account automatically replicate data to another region?

A. Yes

B. No

Answer – A

Explanation:

Create storage account

Basics   Advanced   Tags   Review + create

Azure Storage is a Microsoft-managed service providing cloud storage that is highly available, secure, durable, scalable, and redundant. Azure Storage includes Azure Blobs (objects), Azure Data Lake Storage Gen2, Azure Files, Azure Queues, and Azure Tables. The cost of your storage account depends on the usage and the options you choose below. Learn more

PROJECT DETAILS

Select the subscription to manage deployed resources and costs. Use resource groups like folders to organize and manage all your resources.

* Subscription	Microsoft Azure Sponsorship	⌄
⌐ * Resource group	Select existing...	⌄
	Create new	

INSTANCE DETAILS

The default deployment model is Resource Manager, which supports the latest Azure features. You may choose to deploy using the classic deployment model instead. Choose classic deployment model

* Storage account name ❶		
* Location	(US) East US	⌄
Performance ❶	⦿ Standard ◯ Premium	
Account kind ❶	StorageV2 (general purpose v2)	⌄
Replication ❶	**Read-access geo-redundant storage (RA-GRS)**	⌄
	⌐ **Default Value**	
Access tier (default) ❶	◯ Cool ⦿ Hot	

You need to set the replication strategy in order to make this possible. Below is the table on the redundancy for storage accounts

Scenario	LRS	ZRS	GRS	RA-GRS
Node unavailability within a data center	Yes	Yes	Yes	Yes
An entire data center (zonal or non-zonal) becomes unavailable	No	Yes	Yes	Yes
A region-wide outage	No	No	Yes	Yes

For ensuring data is replicated to another region, you have to choose either Geo redundant storage or Read access geo redundant storage.

For more information on Azure storage redundancy, please visit the below URL

https://docs.microsoft.com/en-us/azure/storage/common/storage-redundancy

65. A company wants to make use of Azure for deployment of various solutions. They want to ensure that suspicious attacks and threats to resources in their Azure account are prevented. Which of the following helps prevent such attacks by using in-built sensors in Azure?

A. Azure AD Identity Protection
B. Azure DDoS attacks
C. Azure privileged identity management
D. Azure Advanced Threat protection

Answer – D

Explanation:

The Microsoft documentation states the below feature on the Azure Advanced Threat protection service

Monitor and profile user behavior and activities

Azure ATP monitors and analyzes user activities and information across your network, such as permissions and group membership, creating a behavioral baseline for each user. Azure ATP then identifies anomalies with adaptive built-in intelligence, giving you insights into suspicious activities and events, revealing the advanced threats, compromised users, and insider threats facing your organization. Azure ATP's proprietary sensors monitor organizational domain controllers, providing a comprehensive view for all user activities from every device.

Options A and C are incorrect since these are used for protecting identities in Azure AD

Option B is incorrect since this is a solely a solution to protect against DDoS attacks

For more information on Azure Advanced Thread protection, please visit the below URL

https://docs.microsoft.com/en-us/azure-advanced-threat-protection/what-is-atp

66. A company is planning on hosting resources in Azure. They want to ensure that Azure complies with the rules and regulations of the region for hosting resources. Which of the following can assist the company in getting the required compliance reports?

A. Azure AD
B. Microsoft Trust Center
C. Azure Advisor
D. Azure Security Center

Answer – B

Explanation:

The Microsoft documentation mentions below on what are the services offered by the Microsoft Trust Center

Here's what you find at the Microsoft Trust Center:

- Security – Learn how all the Microsoft Cloud services are secured.
- Privacy – Understand how Microsoft ensures privacy of your Data in the Microsoft cloud.
- Compliance – Discover how Microsoft helps organizations comply with national, regional, and industry-specific requirements governing the collection and use of individuals' data.
- Transparency – View how Microsoft believes that you control your data in the cloud and how Microsoft helps you know as much as possible about how that data is handled.
- Products and Services – See all the Microsoft Cloud products and services in one place
- Service Trust Portal – Obtain copies of independent audit reports of Microsoft cloud services, risk assessments, security best practices, and related materials.
- What's New – Find out what's new in Microsoft Cloud Trust
- Resources – Investigate white papers, videos, and case studies on Microsoft Trusted Cloud

The Microsoft Trust Center has what you need to understand what we do to secure the Microsoft Cloud.

Option A is incorrect since this is used for identity management

Option C is incorrect since this is used to provide recommendations in Azure

Option D is incorrect since this is a unified infrastructure security management system in Azure

For more information on Microsoft Trust Center, please visit the below URL

https://docs.microsoft.com/en-us/azure/security/security-microsoft-trust-center

67. A company has just deployed a Virtual Machine named demovm to Azure. The overview of the Virtual Machine is shown below.

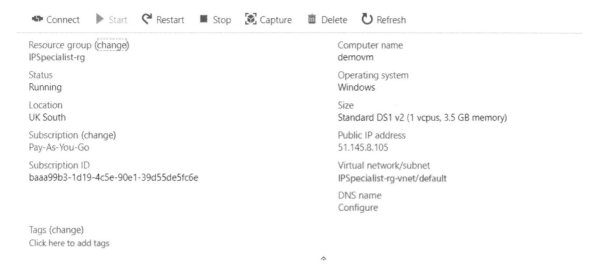

The company needs to know if the underlying infrastructure in Azure hosting the Virtual Machine has any issues? Where could they view such issues?

    A. Azure Advisor

    B. Azure AD

    C. The Virtual Machine blade

    D. Azure Monitor

Answer – C

Explanation:

You can see for any service health issues for the infrastructure of the Virtual Machine in the VM blade itself. Just go to Resource health as shown below

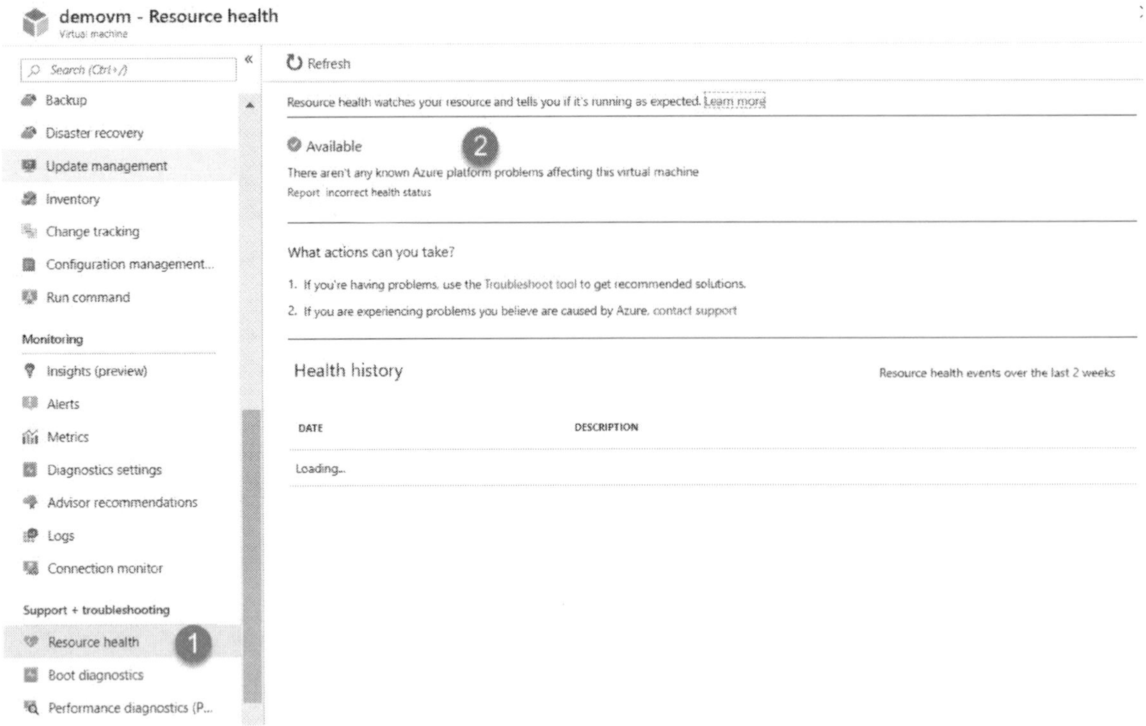

Option A is incorrect since this is used to provide recommendations in Azure

Option B is incorrect since this is used for identity management

Option D is incorrect since will give you the health of the entire Azure Infrastructure but will not specifically let you know on the infrastructure health for just the Virtual Machine.

For more information on Azure resource health, please visit the below URL

https://docs.microsoft.com/en-us/azure/service-health/resource-health-overview

68. A company is planning on hosting 2 Virtual Machines in Azure as shown below

Virtual Machine Name	Virtual Machine Size	Region
demovm	B1S	East US 2
demovm1	B1S	West Central US

Would both the Virtual Machines always generate the same monthly costs?

A. Yes

B. No

Answer – B

Explanation:

The costing for Virtual Machine depends on the region where it is hosted

Below is a screenshot from the link given below where the pricing for a Virtual Machine changes as the region value changes

https://azure.microsoft.com/en-in/pricing/details/virtual-machines/windows/

OS/Software: Windows OS   Region: East US 2   Currency: Indian Rupee (₹)   Display pricing by: Hour

Category: All   General purpose   Compute optimised   Memory optimised   Storage optimised   GPU   High performance compute

Bs-series

Bs-series are economical virtual machines that provide a low-cost option for workloads that typically run at a low to moderate baseline CPU performance, but sometimes need to burst to significantly higher CPU performance when the demand rises. These workloads do not require the use of the full CPU all the time, but occasionally will need to burst to finish some tasks more quickly. Many applications such as development and test servers, low traffic web servers, small databases, micro services, servers for proof-of-concepts, build servers and code repositories fit into this model.

SHOW AZURE HYBRID BENEFIT PRICING

Add to estimate	Instance	vCPU(s)	RAM	Temporary storage	Pay as you go with AHB	1 year reserved with AHB (% Savings)	3 year reserved with AHB (% Savings)	Spot with AHB (% Savings)
+	B1S	1	1 GiB	4 GiB	₹0.6875/hour	₹0.3999/hour (~42%)	₹0.2591/hour (~62%)	– –

OS/Software: Windows OS   Region: West Central US   Currency: Indian Rupee (₹)   Display pricing by: Hour

Category: All   General purpose   Compute optimised   Memory optimised   Storage optimised   GPU   High performance compute

Bs-series

Bs-series are economical virtual machines that provide a low-cost option for workloads that typically run at a low to moderate baseline CPU performance, but sometimes need to burst to significantly higher CPU performance when the demand rises. These workloads do not require the use of the full CPU all the time, but occasionally will need to burst to finish some tasks more quickly. Many applications such as development and test servers, low traffic web servers, small databases, micro services, servers for proof-of-concepts, build servers and code repositories fit into this model.

SHOW AZURE HYBRID BENEFIT PRICING

Add to estimate	Instance	vCPU(s)	RAM	Temporary storage	Pay as you go with AHB	1 year reserved with AHB (% Savings)	3 year reserved with AHB (% Savings)	Spot with AHB (% Savings)
+	B1S	1	1 GiB	4 GiB	₹0.8263/hour	₹0.4832/hour (~42%)	₹0.3120/hour (~62%)	– –

For more information on the pricing calculator, please visit the below URL

https://azure.microsoft.com/en-us/pricing/calculator/

69. A company has a set of resources deployed to Azure. They want to make use of the Azure Advisor tool. Would the Azure Advisor tool give recommendations on how to configure Virtual Network settings?

A. Yes

B. No

Answer – B

Explanation:

If you see the Azure Advisor as shown below, the main area recommendations are High Availability, Security, Performance and Cost.

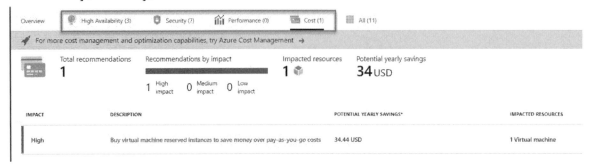

| Overview | High Availability (3) | Security (7) | Performance (0) | Cost (1) | All (11) |

For more cost management and optimization capabilities, try Azure Cost Management →

Total recommendations	Recommendations by impact	Impacted resources	Potential yearly savings
1	1 High impact 0 Medium impact 0 Low impact	1	34 USD

IMPACT	DESCRIPTION	POTENTIAL YEARLY SAVINGS*	IMPACTED RESOURCES
High	Buy virtual machine reserved instances to save money over pay-as-you-go costs	34.44 USD	1 Virtual machine

For more information on Azure Advisor, please visit the below URL

https://docs.microsoft.com/en-us/azure/advisor/advisor-overview

70. A company is planning on deploying resources to Azure. Which of the following in Azure provides a consistent management layer for deploying objects to the Azure Cloud Infrastructure?

A. Azure Resource Groups

B. Azure policies

C. Azure Management Groups

D. Azure Resource Manager

Answer – D

Explanation:

The Microsoft documentation mentions the following

Azure Resource Manager overview

02/01/2019 · 11 minutes to read · Contributors 🖧 🖧 🖧 🖧 🖧 all

Azure Resource Manager is the deployment and management service for Azure. It provides a consistent management layer that enables you to create, update, and delete resources in your Azure subscription. You can use its access control, auditing, and tagging features to secure and organize your resources after deployment.

Option A is incorrect since this provides a means to categorize resources deployed to Azure. It's not a platform

Option B is incorrect since this allows you to govern Azure resources

Option C is incorrect since this allows you to efficiently manage access, policies, and compliance for those subscriptions

For more information on Azure Resource Manager, please visit the below URL

https://docs.microsoft.com/en-us/azure/azure-resource-manager/resource-group-overview

71. A company is planning on setting up a solution in Azure. The solution would have the following key requirement
   • Provide a digital online assistant that provides speech support

Which of the following would be best suited for this requirement?
   A. Azure Machine Learning
   B. Azure IoT Hub
   C. Azure AI Bot
   D. Azure Functions

Answer – C

Explanation:

The Microsoft documentation mentions the following

About Azure Bot Service

> ⓘ **Note**
>
> This topic is for the latest release of the SDK (v4). You can find content for the older version of the SDK (v3) here.

Azure Bot Service provides tools to build, test, deploy, and manage intelligent bots all in one place. Through the use of modular and extensible framework provided by the SDK, tools, templates, and AI services developers can create bots that use speech, understand natural language, handle questions and answers, and more.

Since this is a clear feature on the tool, all other options are incorrect

For more information on Azure AI Bot, please visit the below URL

https://docs.microsoft.com/en-us/azure/bot-service/bot-service-overview-introduction?view=azure-bot-service-4.0

72. A company is planning on setting up a solution in Azure. The solution would have the following key requirement
   • Uses past trainings to provide predictions that have high probability

Which of the following would be best suited for this requirement?

A. Azure Machine Learning

B. Azure IoT Hub

C. Azure AI Bot

D. Azure Functions

Answer – A

Explanation:

The Microsoft documentation mentions the following

What is Azure Machine Learning service?

Azure Machine Learning service provides a cloud-based environment you can use to develop, train, test, deploy, manage, and track machine learning models.

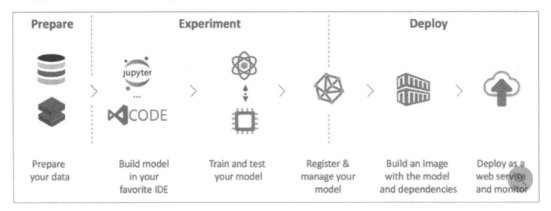

Since this is a clear feature on the tool, all other options are incorrect

For more information on Azure Machine Learning service, please visit the below URL

https://docs.microsoft.com/en-us/azure/machine-learning/service/overview-what-is-azure-ml

73. A company is planning on setting up a solution in Azure. The solution would have the following key requirement

- Provides serverless computing functionalities

Which of the following would be best suited for this requirement?

A. Azure Machine Learning

B. Azure IoT Hub

C. Azure AI Bot

D. Azure Functions

Answer – D

Explanation:

The Microsoft documentation mentions the following

An introduction to Azure Functions

10/03/2017 · 4 minutes to read · Contributors 🔵 🔴 🟢 🔴 🔵 all

Azure Functions is a solution for easily running small pieces of code, or "functions," in the cloud. You can write just the code you need for the problem at hand, without worrying about a whole application or the infrastructure to run it. Functions can make development even more productive, and you can use your development language of choice, such as C#, F#, Node.js, Java, or PHP. Pay only for the time your code runs and trust Azure to scale as needed. Azure Functions lets you develop serverless applications on Microsoft Azure.

Since this is a clear feature on the tool, all other options are incorrect

For more information on Azure Functions, please visit the below URL

https://docs.microsoft.com/en-us/azure/azure-functions/functions-overview

74. A company is planning on setting up a solution in Azure. The solution would have the following key requirement
- Gives the ability to process data from millions of sensors
A. Azure Machine Learning
B. Azure IoT Hub
C. Azure AI Bot
D. Azure Functions

Answer – B

Explanation:

The Microsoft documentation mentions the following

What is Azure IoT Hub?

07/04/2018 · 3 minutes to read · Contributors ⬤ ⬤ ⬤

IoT Hub is a managed service, hosted in the cloud, that acts as a central message hub for bi-directional communication between your IoT application and the devices it manages. You can use Azure IoT Hub to build IoT solutions with reliable and secure communications between millions of IoT devices and a cloud-hosted solution backend. You can connect virtually any device to IoT Hub.

Since this is a clear feature on the tool, all other options are incorrect

For more information on Azure IoT Hub, please visit the below URL

https://docs.microsoft.com/en-us/azure/iot-hub/about-iot-hub

75. A company has a number of resources hosted in Azure. They want to have a comprehensive solution for collecting, analyzing, and acting on telemetry from your cloud. Which of the following service would you use for this requirement?

A. Azure Event Hubs

B. Azure Analysis Services

C. Azure Advisor

D. Azure Monitor

Answer – D

Explanation:

Azure Monitor maximizes the availability and performance of your applications and services by delivering a comprehensive solution for collecting, analyzing, and acting on telemetry from your cloud and on-premises environments. It helps you understand how your applications are performing and proactively identifies issues affecting them and the resources they depend on.

For more information on Azure Monitor, please visit the below URL

https://docs.microsoft.com/en-us/azure/azure-monitor/overview

You can use Azure Monitor to collect all the data from various sources as shown below. You can then perform interactive queries on the stored logs.

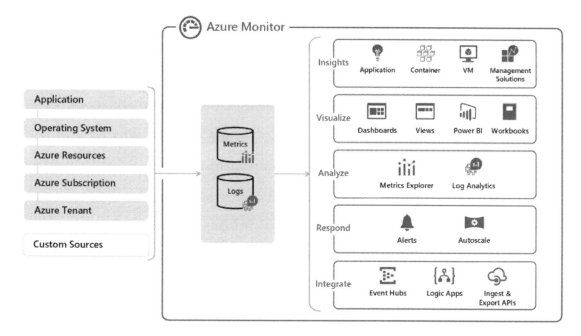

Option A is incorrect since this service is a big data streaming platform and event ingestion service

Option B is incorrect since this is a fully managed platform as a service (PaaS) that provides enterprise-grade data models in the cloud.

Option C is incorrect since this is used as a recommendation's engine

76. A company has a virtual machine defined as demovm. This Virtual Machine was created with the standard settings. An application is installed on demovm. It now needs to be ensured that the application can be accessed over the Internet via HTTP.

You propose the solution to modify the DDoS protection plan

Would this solution fit the requirement?

   A. Yes
   B. No

Answer – B

Explanation:

This service is specifically meant to protect your resources against a DDoS attack and not allow traffic into the Virtual machine

For more information on DDoS protection, please visit the below URL

https://docs.microsoft.com/en-us/azure/virtual-network/ddos-protection-overview

77. A company has a virtual machine defined as demovm. This Virtual Machine was created with the standard settings. An application is installed on demovm. It now needs to be ensured that the application can be accessed over the Internet via HTTP using prioritized security rules and port ranges

You make modifications to the Azure firewall

Would this solution fit the requirement?

A. Yes

B. No

Answer – B

Explanation:

For information on Security Groups, please visit the below URL

https://docs.microsoft.com/en-us/azure/virtual-network/security-overview

Security rules

A network security group contains zero, or as many rules as desired, within Azure subscription limits. Each rule specifies the following properties:

Property	Explanation
Name	A unique name within the network security group.
Priority	A number between 100 and 4096. Rules are processed in priority order, with lower numbers processed before higher numbers, because lower numbers have higher priority. Once traffic matches a rule, processing stops. As a result, any rules that exist with lower priorities (higher numbers) that have the same attributes as rules with higher priorities are not processed.

The question is asking for "using prioritized security rules and port ranges". Please note that "prioritized security rules" can only be added through a "security group". Through the Azure Firewall we can only add normal security rules but we CANNOT "prioritize" the security rules

For more information on Azure Firewall, please visit the below URL

https://docs.microsoft.com/en-us/azure/firewall/overview

What is Azure Firewall?

11/19/2019 • 8 minutes to read • 🔵 🔵 🔵 🔵 🔵

Azure Firewall is a managed, cloud-based network security service that protects your Azure Virtual Network resources. It's a fully stateful firewall as a service with built-in high availability and unrestricted cloud scalability.

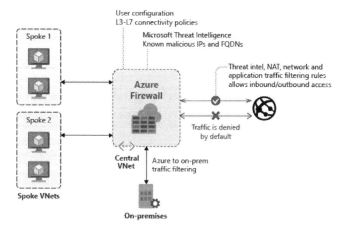

You can centrally create, enforce, and log application and network connectivity policies across subscriptions and virtual networks. Azure Firewall uses a static public IP address for your virtual network resources allowing outside firewalls to identify traffic originating from your virtual network. The service is fully integrated with Azure Monitor for

---

78. A company has a virtual machine defined as demovm. This Virtual Machine was created with the standard settings. An application is installed on demovm. It now needs to be ensured that the application can be accessed over the Internet via HTTP.

You modify the Azure Traffic Manager profile

Would this solution fit the requirement?

A. Yes

B. No

Answer – B

Explanation:

The Azure Traffic Manager is a DNS-based traffic load balancer

For more information on Azure Traffic Manager, please visit the below URL

https://docs.microsoft.com/en-us/azure/traffic-manager/traffic-manager-overview

79. A company has a virtual machine defined as demovm. This Virtual Machine was created with the standard settings. Now this virtual machine needs to communicate with other Azure resources within the Virtual Network

You modify the Network Security Groups

Would this solution fit the requirement?

    A. Yes

    B. No

Answer – A

Explanation:

You should change the Network Security group by adding a rule for allowing Inbound Traffic as shown below

1. Create an Inbound Network Security Rule
2. Ensure the Service Tag is the Internet
3. Ensure the destination port range is 80
4. Ensure the Action is placed as Allow

For more information on Virtual Network Security, please visit the below URL

https://docs.microsoft.com/en-us/azure/virtual-network/security-overview

80. A company is looking at the possibility of using Azure Government for development of their cloud-based solutions. Which of the following customers are allowed to use Azure Government? Choose 2 answers from the options given below

A. A Canadian government contractor

B. A European government contractor

C. A United States government entity

D. A United States government contractor

E. A European government entity

Answer - C and D

Explanation:

This is given in the Microsoft documentation

What is Azure Government?

09/17/2018 · 2 minutes to read · Contributors 🔵 ⚫ 🔴

US government agencies or their partners interested in cloud services that meet government security and compliance requirements, can be confident that Microsoft Azure Government provides world-class security, protection, and compliance services. Azure Government delivers a dedicated cloud enabling government agencies and their partners to transform mission-critical workloads to the cloud. Azure Government services handle data that is subject to certain government regulations and requirements, such as FedRAMP, NIST 800.171 (DIB), ITAR, IRS 1075, DoD L4, and CJIS. In order to provide you with the highest level of security and compliance, Azure Government uses physically isolated datacenters and networks (located in U.S. only).

Azure Government customers (US federal, state, and local government or their partners) are subject to validation of eligibility. If there is a question about eligibility for Azure Government, you should consult your account team. To sign up for trial, request your trial subscription.

Since this is clearly given in the Microsoft documentation, all other options are incorrect

For more information on Azure Government, please visit the below URL

https://docs.microsoft.com/en-us/azure/azure-government/documentation-government-welcome

81. A company plans to purchase an Azure Support plan. Below is a key requirement for the support plan

• Ensure that for high severity cases, there is a response within 10 minutes

A recommendation is made to purchase the Basic Support plan

Would this recommendation fulfil the requirement?

A. Yes

B. No

Answer – B

Explanation:

As per the support plans, you can see that the Basic support plan has no SLA in place

	BASIC	DEVELOPER	STANDARD	PROFESSIONAL DIRECT	PREMIER
		Purchase support	Purchase support	Purchase support	Contact Premier
Who Can Open Cases		Unlimited contacts / unlimited cases	Unlimited contacts / unlimited cases	Unlimited contacts / unlimited cases	Unlimited contacts / unlimited cases
Third-Party Software Support		Interoperability & configuration guidance and troubleshooting	Interoperability & configuration guidance and troubleshooting	Interoperability & configuration guidance and troubleshooting	Interoperability & configuration guidance and troubleshooting
Case Severity/Response Times		Minimal business impact (Sev C): <8 business hours[1]	Minimal business impact (Sev C): <8 business hours[1]	Minimal business impact (Sev C): <4 business hours[1]	Minimal business impact (Sev C): <4 business hours[1]
			Moderate business impact (Sev B): <4 hours	Moderate business impact (Sev B): <2 hours	Moderate business impact (Sev B): <2 hours
			Critical business impact (Sev A): <1 hour	Critical business impact (Sev A): <1 hour	Critical business impact (Sev A): <1 hour <15 minutes (with Azure Rapid Response or Azure Event Management)

No SLA

For more information on the support plans, please visit the below URL

https://azure.microsoft.com/en-us/support/plans/

82. A company plans to purchase an Azure Support plan. Below is a key requirement for the support plan

- Ensure that for high severity cases, there is a response within 10 minutes

A recommendation is made to purchase the Professional Direct Support plan

Would this recommendation fulfil the requirement?

A. Yes
B. No

Answer – B

Explanation:

As per the support plans, you can see that the Professional Direct support plan has an SLA of 1 hour for Critical business impact cases.

This means that the response time for high severity cases may be within an hour and not strictly within 10 minutes as per the requirement given in the question

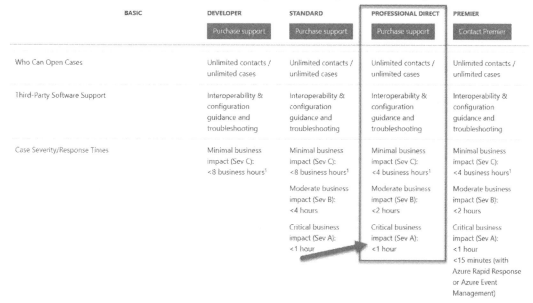

	BASIC	DEVELOPER	STANDARD	PROFESSIONAL DIRECT	PREMIER
		Purchase support	Purchase support	Purchase support	Contact Premier
Who Can Open Cases		Unlimited contacts / unlimited cases	Unlimited contacts / unlimited cases	Unlimited contacts / unlimited cases	Unlimited contacts / unlimited cases
Third-Party Software Support		Interoperability & configuration guidance and troubleshooting	Interoperability & configuration guidance and troubleshooting	Interoperability & configuration guidance and troubleshooting	Interoperability & configuration guidance and troubleshooting
Case Severity/Response Times		Minimal business impact (Sev C): <8 business hours[1]	Minimal business impact (Sev C): <8 business hours[1]	Minimal business impact (Sev C): <4 business hours[1]	Minimal business impact (Sev C): <4 business hours[1]
			Moderate business impact (Sev B): <4 hours	Moderate business impact (Sev B): <2 hours	Moderate business impact (Sev B): <2 hours
			Critical business impact (Sev A): <1 hour	Critical business impact (Sev A): <1 hour	Critical business impact (Sev A): <1 hour <15 minutes (with Azure Rapid Response or Azure Event Management)

For more information on the support plans, please visit the below URL

https://azure.microsoft.com/en-us/support/plans/

83. A company plans to purchase an Azure Support plan. Below is a key requirement for the support plan

- Ensure that for high severity cases, the response is within 15 minutes

A recommendation is made to purchase the Premier Support plan.

Would this recommendation fulfil the requirement?

   A. Yes

   B. No

Answer – A

Explanation:

As per the support plans, you can see that the Premier support plan does provide an initial SLA of 15 minutes for business critical cases

	BASIC	DEVELOPER	STANDARD	PROFESSIONAL DIRECT	PREMIER
		Purchase support	Purchase support	Purchase support	Contact Premier
Who Can Open Cases		Unlimited contacts / unlimited cases	Unlimited contacts / unlimited cases	Unlimited contacts / unlimited cases	Unlimited contacts / unlimited cases
Third-Party Software Support		Interoperability & configuration guidance and troubleshooting	Interoperability & configuration guidance and troubleshooting	Interoperability & configuration guidance and troubleshooting	Interoperability & configuration guidance and troubleshooting
Case Severity/Response Times		Minimal business impact (Sev C): <8 business hours[1]	Minimal business impact (Sev C): <8 business hours[1] Moderate business impact (Sev B): <4 hours Critical business impact (Sev A): <1 hour	Minimal business impact (Sev C): <4 business hours[1] Moderate business impact (Sev B): <2 hours Critical business impact (Sev A): <1 hour	Minimal business impact (Sev C): <4 business hours[1] Moderate business impact (Sev B): <2 hours Critical business impact (Sev A): <1 hour <15 minutes (with Azure Rapid Response or Azure Event Management)

For more information on the support plans, please visit the below URL

https://azure.microsoft.com/en-us/support/plans/

84. A company is planning on deploying a web server and database server as shown in the architecture diagram below. You have to ensure that traffic restrictions are in place so that the database server can only communicate with the web server.

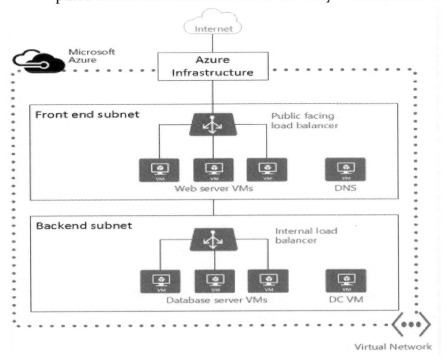

Which of the following would you recommend for implementing these restrictions?

A. Network security groups (NSGs)

B. Azure Service Bus

C. A local network gateway

D. A Virtual Private Gateway

Answer – A

Explanation:

You should use network security groups to allow or deny traffic within subnets.

Below is what the Microsoft documentation mentions in terms of filtering of network traffic

Traffic filtering

- You can filter network traffic between resources in a virtual network using a network security group, an NVA that filters network traffic, or both. To deploy an NVA, such as a firewall, to filter network traffic, see the Azure Marketplace. When using an NVA, you also create custom routes to route traffic from subnets to the NVA. Learn more about traffic routing.
- A network security group contains several default security rules that allow or deny traffic to or from resources. A network security group can be associated to a network interface, the subnet the network interface is in, or both. To simplify management of security rules, it's recommended that you associate a network security group to individual subnets, rather than individual network interfaces within the subnet, whenever possible.
- If different VMs within a subnet need different security rules applied to them, you can associate the network interface in the VM to one or more application security groups. A security rule can specify an application security group in its source, destination, or both. That rule then only applies to the network interfaces that are members of the application security group. Learn more about network security groups and application security groups.
- Azure creates several default security rules within each network security group. One default rule allows all traffic to flow between all resources in a virtual network. To override this behavior, use network security groups, custom routing to route traffic to an NVA, or both. It's recommended that you familiarize yourself with all of Azure's default security rules and understand how network security group rules are applied to a resource.

- Option B is incorrect since this is used as a messaging system
- Option C is incorrect since this is used to represent a VPN device in a Site-to-Site VPN connection
- Option D is incorrect since this is normally used to connect networks together via the Internet

- For more information on network planning and design, please visit the below URL
  - https://docs.microsoft.com/en-us/azure/virtual-network/virtual-network-vnet-plan-design-arm

85. A company wants to make use of an Azure service in private preview. Are Azure services in private preview available to all customers?

A. Yes

B. No

Answer – B

Explanation:

Services in private preview are only available upon request. An example is given below. If you go to the services available in beta phase and click on "Try it"

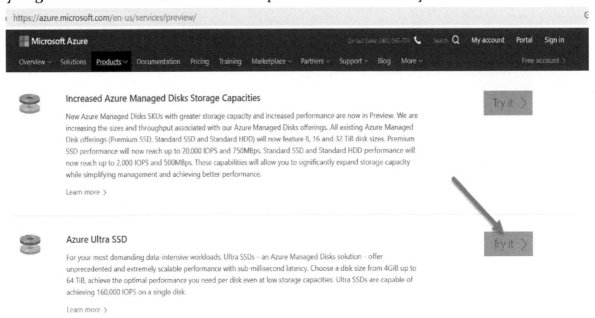

You will be directed to complete a form to avail the preview of the service.

Ultra SSD Disks - Preview

Thank you for your interest in participating in the Ultra SSD Disks limited Public Preview.

Overview:

Ultra SSD is a new Azure Managed Disk offering for your most latency-sensitive and high IOPS workloads. Ultra SSDs deliver unprecedented and extremely scalable performance with sub-millisecond latency:
- Choose a disk size from 4GiB up to 64TiB
- Achieve the optimal performance you need per disk even at low storage capacities
- Scale performance beyond 80000 IOPS and throughput up to 2 GB/s per disk without restarting your virtual machines using our flexible and innovative architecture

Ultra SSDs are currently available in our East US 2 Region.

To leverage the full capabilities of Ultra SSDs, we are also introducing a new VM Size as part of this preview that will allow you to reach up to 160K storage IOPS.

Please complete the signup survey questions below. We will review all responses and will reach out to you if we have any additional questions.

* Required

1. Your full name *

Enter your answer

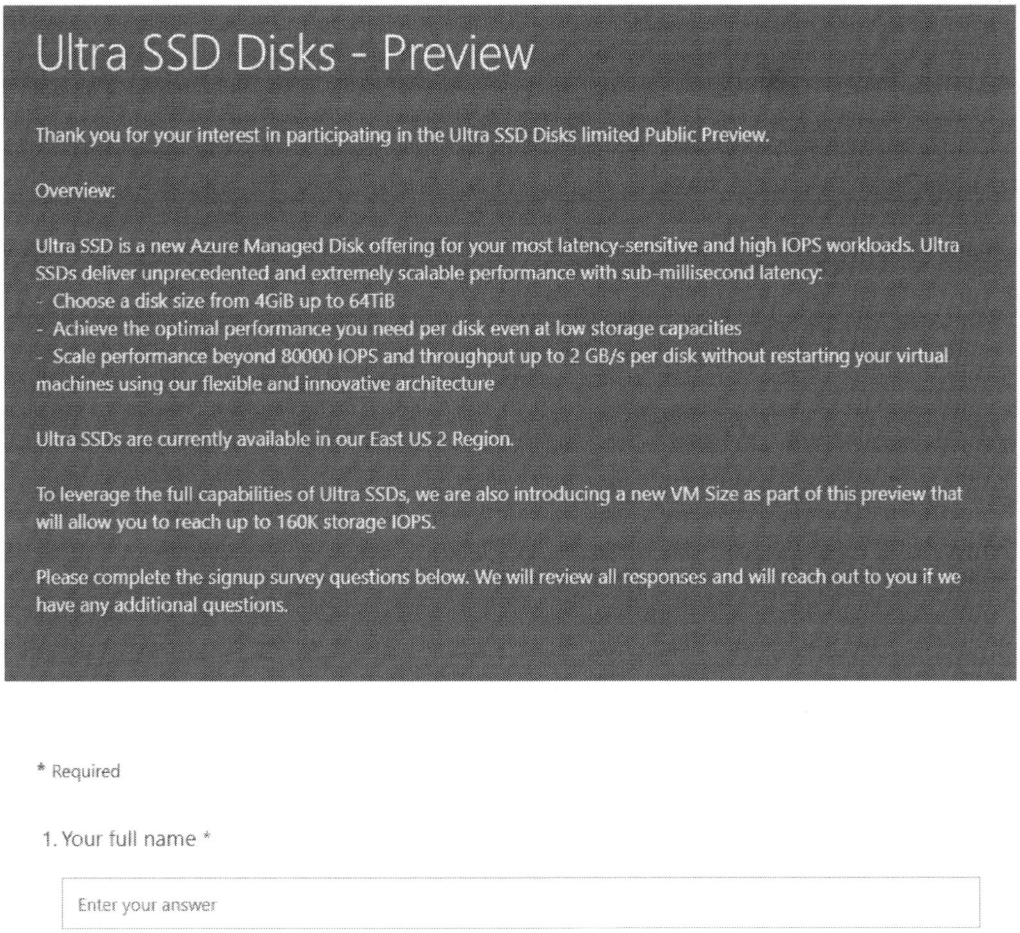

For more information on services in beta test phase, please visit the below URL
https://azure.microsoft.com/en-us/services/preview/

86. A company wants to make use of an Azure service in public preview. Are Azure services in public preview available to all customers?

A. Yes

B. No

Answer – A

Explanation:
An example is given below. Here there is a preview available for Virtual Machines in Azure Monitor.

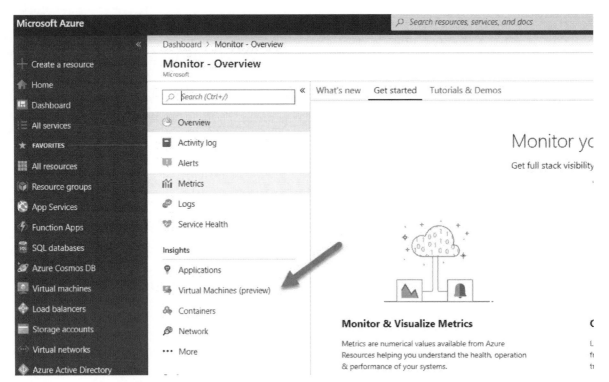

For more information on updates to the Azure platform, please visit the below URL

https://azure.microsoft.com/en-us/updates

87. A company is planning on setting up an Azure account. Can they purchase multiple Azure subscriptions and associate all subscriptions to a single Azure?

A. Yes

B. No

Answer – A

Explanation:

Yes, you can have multiple subscriptions against a single AD tenant as shown below in the Microsoft documentation

Figure 3: Multiple subscriptions of an organization that use the same Azure AD tenant

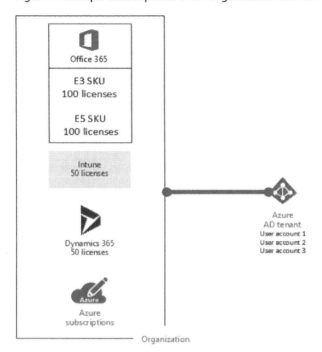

- For more information on subscriptions, licenses and tenants please visit the below URL
  - https://docs.microsoft.com/en-us/office365/enterprise/subscriptions-licenses-accounts-and-tenants-for-microsoft-cloud-offerings

88. Your company has multiple subscriptions in Azure and the administrators want to transfer billing ownership of the subscriptions between your company's accounts

Does your administrator need to contact Microsoft for this activity?

A. Yes

B. No

Answer – B

Explanation:

Ideally you would look to transfer subscriptions under one account and manage them centrally. If you go to your subscription, there will be a Transfer subscription option as shown below

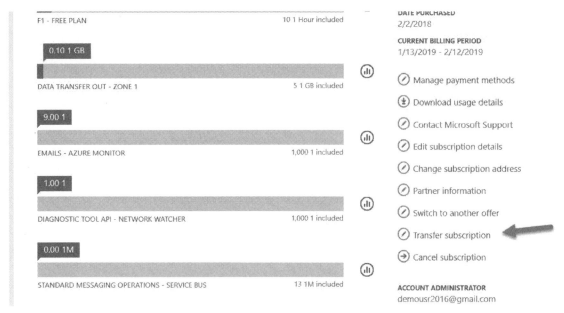

For more information on transferring subscriptions please visit the below URL

- https://docs.microsoft.com/en-us/azure/billing/billing-subscription-transfer

89. A company has multiple subscriptions. They want to create resources in different subscriptions. Is it possible to create resources in different subscriptions?

A. Yes

B. No

Answer – A

Explanation:

An example of this is given below. Here we have 2 storage accounts created in one Azure account, under multiple subscriptions

For more information on Azure resource manager, please visit the below URL

https://docs.microsoft.com/en-us/azure/azure-resource-manager/resource-group-overview

90. A company is planning on setting up a solution in Azure. The solution would have the following key requirement
- Provide an analytics service for BI and machine learning needs

Which of the following would be best suited for this requirement?

A. Azure Content Delivery Network

B. Azure Synapse

C. Azure Load Balancer

D. Azure Cosmos DB

Answer – B

Explanation:

The Microsoft documentation mentions the following

What is Azure Synapse Analytics (formerly SQL DW)?

11/04/2019 • 2 minutes to read • 🞄🞄🞄🞄🞄 +12

Azure Synapse is a limitless analytics service that brings together enterprise data warehousing and Big Data analytics. It gives you the freedom to query data on your terms, using either serverless on-demand or provisioned resources—at scale. Azure Synapse brings these two worlds together with a unified experience to ingest, prepare, manage, and serve data for immediate BI and machine learning needs

Azure Synapse has four components:

- SQL Analytics: Complete T-SQL based analytics – Generally Available
  - SQL pool (pay per DWU provisioned)
  - SQL on-demand (pay per TB processed) – (Preview)
- Spark: Deeply integrated Apache Spark (Preview)
- Data Integration: Hybrid data integration (Preview)
- Studio: Unified user experience. (Preview)

For more information on the Azure Synapse service, please visit the below URL

- https://docs.microsoft.com/en-us/azure/sql-data-warehouse/sql-data-warehouse-overview-what-is

91. A company is planning on setting up a solution in Azure. The solution would have the following key requirement

- Provide an efficient way to distribute web content to users across the world

Which of the following would be best suited for this requirement?

A. Azure Content Delivery Network

B. Azure SQL Datawarehouse

C. Azure Load Balancer

D. Azure HD Insight

Answer – A

Explanation:

The Microsoft documentation mentions the following

What is a content delivery network on Azure?

05/09/2018 • 3 minutes to read • Contributors 🐶 🌐 🕸 🐕 ❄ all

A content delivery network (CDN) is a distributed network of servers that can efficiently deliver web content to users. CDNs store cached content on edge servers in point-of-presence (POP) locations that are close to end users, to minimize latency.

Azure Content Delivery Network (CDN) offers developers a global solution for rapidly delivering high-bandwidth content to users by caching their content at strategically placed physical nodes across the world. Azure CDN can also accelerate dynamic content, which cannot be cached, by leveraging various network optimizations using CDN POPs. For example, route optimization to bypass Border Gateway Protocol (BGP).

The benefits of using Azure CDN to deliver web site assets include:

- Better performance and improved user experience for end users, especially when using applications in which multiple round-trips are required to load content.
- Large scaling to better handle instantaneous high loads, such as the start of a product launch event.
- Distribution of user requests and serving of content directly from edge servers so that less traffic is sent to the origin server.

Since this is a clear feature on the tool, all other options are incorrect

For more information on Azure Content Delivery, please visit the below URL

https://docs.microsoft.com/en-us/azure/cdn/cdn-overview

92. A company is planning on setting up a solution in Azure. The solution would have the following key requirement

Provide the ability to distribute user traffic to a set of backend Virtual Machines

A. Azure Content Delivery Network

B. Azure SQL Datawarehouse

C. Azure Load Balancer

D. Azure HD Insight

Answer – C

Explanation:

The Microsoft documentation mentions the following

What is Azure Load Balancer?

01/11/2019 · 15 minutes to read · Contributors 🌑 ⬤ ◉ 🌗 ◉ all

With Azure Load Balancer, you can scale your applications and create high availability for your services. Load Balancer supports inbound and outbound scenarios, provides low latency and high throughput, and scales up to millions of flows for all TCP and UDP applications.

Load Balancer distributes new inbound flows that arrive on the Load Balancer's frontend to backend pool instances, according to rules and health probes.

Additionally, a public Load Balancer can provide outbound connections for virtual machines (VMs) inside your virtual network by translating their private IP addresses to public IP addresses.

Azure Load Balancer is available in two SKUs: Basic and Standard. There are differences in scale, features, and pricing. Any scenario that's possible with Basic Load Balancer can also be created with Standard Load Balancer, although the approaches might differ slightly. As you learn about Load Balancer, it is important to familiarize yourself with the fundamentals and SKU-specific differences.

Since this is a clear feature on the tool, all other options are incorrect

For more information on Azure Load Balancer, please visit the below URL

https://docs.microsoft.com/en-us/azure/load-balancer/load-balancer-overview

93. A company is planning on setting up a solution in Azure. The solution would have the following key requirement

Provide a cloud service that makes it easy, fast, and cost-effective to analyse streaming data.

Which of the following Azure services would meet the criteria?

A. Azure Content Delivery Network

B. Azure SQL Datawarehouse

C. Azure Load Balancer

D. Azure HD Insight

Answer – D

Explanation:

The Microsoft documentation mentions the following

Azure HDInsight Documentation

Learn how to use Azure HDInsight to analyze streaming or historical data. Tutorials and other documentation show you how to create clusters, process and analyze big data, and develop solutions using the most popular open-source frameworks, like Apache Hadoop, Apache Spark, Apache Hive, Apache LLAP, Apache Kafka, Apache Storm, and Microsoft Machine Learning Server.

Azure HDInsight is a fully managed, full-spectrum, open-source analytics service for enterprises. HDInsight is a cloud service that makes it easy, fast, and cost-effective to process massive amounts of data. HDInsight also supports a broad range of scenarios, like extract, transform, and load (ETL); data warehousing; machine learning; and IoT.

Since this is a clear feature on the tool, all other options are incorrect

For more information on Azure HDInsight, please visit the below URL

- https://docs.microsoft.com/en-us/azure/hdinsight/

Ask our Experts

94. A company is planning on hosting a set of resources in their Azure subscription. They are currently aware that most Azure Service can provide an SLA of 99.9%. Which of the following technique could be used to increase the uptime for resources hosted in Azure?

A. Adding resources to multiple regions

B. Adding resources to the same data center

C. Adding resources to the same resource group

D. Adding resources to the same subscription

Answer – A

Explanation:

By having an additional region for your resources, you have more options if the primary regions go down for any reason. This can increase the availability of your entire application and hence give a better uptime on the SLA.

An example architecture of a highly available architecture for a web application is shown below

This is from the Microsoft documentation

Run a web application in multiple Azure regions for high availability

10/25/2018 · 8 minutes to read · Contributors 👤👤👤👤👤 all

This reference architecture shows how to run an Azure App Service application in multiple regions to achieve high availability.

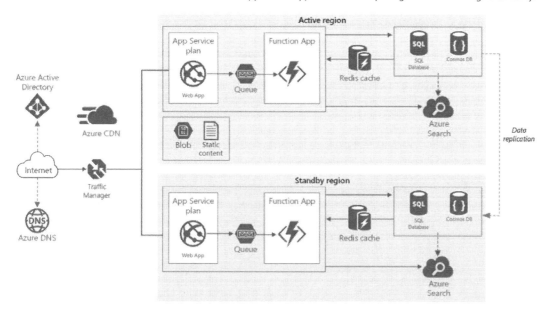

All other options are invalid, because the best-case scenario is to split resources across different availability zones or regions.

For more information on an example for high availability for your application, please visit the below URL

https://docs.microsoft.com/en-us/azure/architecture/reference-architectures/app-service-web-app/multi-region

95. A company is planning on using Azure Cloud for hosting resources. Which of the following is a key advantage of hosting resources in the Azure public cloud?

A. All users across the world can access the resources in your Azure account

B. High reliability - a vast network of servers ensures against failure

C. Only privileged users can have access to resources in your Azure account

D. You pay a capital upfront cost when using resources in the public cloud

Answer – B

Explanation:

What is a public cloud?

Public clouds are the most common way of deploying cloud computing. The cloud resources (like servers and storage) are owned and operated by a third-party cloud service provider and delivered over the Internet. Microsoft Azure is an example of a public cloud. With a public cloud, all hardware, software and other supporting infrastructure is owned and managed by the cloud provider. In a public cloud, you share the same hardware, storage and network devices with other organisations or cloud "tenants." You access services and manage your account using a web browser. Public cloud deployments are frequently used to provide web-based email, online office applications, storage and testing and development environments.

Advantages of public clouds:

- Lower costs—no need to purchase hardware or software and you pay only for the service you use.
- No maintenance—your service provider provides the maintenance.
- Near-unlimited scalability—on-demand resources are available to meet your business needs.
- High reliability—a vast network of servers ensures against failure.

- Reference URL
  - https://azure.microsoft.com/en-in/overview/what-are-private-public-hybrid-clouds/

96. A company needs to deploy several virtual machines. Each of these virtual machines will have the same set of permissions. To minimize the administrative overhead, in which would you deploy the Azure Virtual Machines?

A. Azure policies
B. Azure Virtual Machine Scale sets
C. Azure Resource Groups
D. Azure Tags

Answer – C

Explanation:

When you deploy a resource to a resource group which has a set of permissions defined, the resource will inherit the permissions assigned to the resource group. An example is shown below.

1. An example is shown below where a resource group has a permission defined.

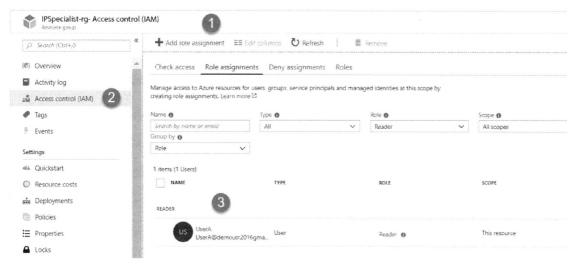

1. And there is a resource defined in the resource group

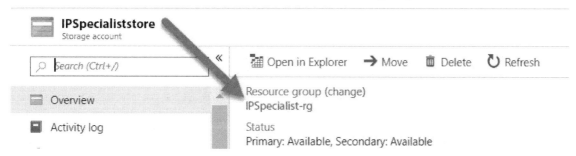

1. If you go to the Access Control section of the resource, you will see that the permissions is inherited from the resource group.

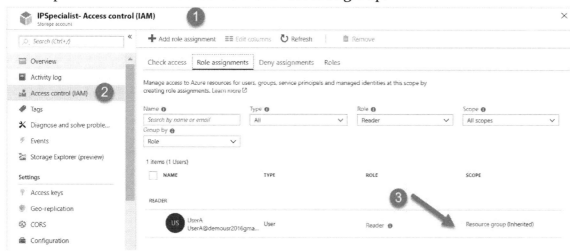

For more information on role-based access control, please visit the below URL

- https://docs.microsoft.com/en-us/azure/role-based-access-control/role-assignments-portal

97. An application consists of a set of virtual machines hosted in a Virtual Network. In a month, the application seems to have a load of around 20% for 3 weeks. During the last week the load on the application reaches 80%. Which of the following concept would you implement to ensure that cost and efficiency of the underlying application infrastructure?

A. High availability

B. Elasticity

C. Disaster recovery

D. Fault tolerance

Answer – B

Explanation:

Here the concept refers to Elasticity.

- In this use case, you could define a Virtual Machine Scale set in Azure
- You could define an initial set of Virtual Machines as part of the scale set that would run for the first 3 weeks.
- You can then add a scaling policy to add more Virtual Machines to support the application during the last week
- You can then add a scaling policy to remove the extra Virtual Machines at the end of last week to save on costs

All other options are incorrect since they all refer to availability of the infrastructure.

For more information on Virtual Machine scale sets, please visit the below URL

https://docs.microsoft.com/en-us/azure/virtual-machine-scale-sets/overview

98. A company wants to start using Azure. They want to make use of availability zones in Azure. Which of the following is attached to the concept of availability zones in Azure?

A. Region failure

B. Resource failure

C. Data Center failure

D. Azure failure

Answer – C

Explanation:

The Microsoft documentation mentions the following

What are Availability Zones in Azure?

08/31/2018 • 2 minutes to read • Contributors 🌐 👤 👥 𝒜 👥 all

Availability Zones is a high-availability offering that protects your applications and data from datacenter failures. Availability Zones are unique physical locations within an Azure region. Each zone is made up of one or more datacenters equipped with independent power, cooling, and networking. To ensure resiliency, there's a minimum of three separate zones in all enabled regions. The physical separation of Availability Zones within a region protects applications and data from datacenter failures. Zone-redundant services replicate your applications and data across Availability Zones to protect from single-points-of-failure. With Availability Zones, Azure offers industry best 99.99% VM uptime SLA. The full Azure SLA explains the guaranteed availability of Azure as a whole.

Since this is clearly mentioned in the Microsoft documentation, all other options are incorrect

For more information on availability zones, please visit the below URL

https://docs.microsoft.com/en-us/azure/availability-zones/az-overview

99. A company wants to start using Azure. They want to make use of availability zones in Azure. If they deploy resources across all regions in Azure, can they make use of availability zones in all regions in Azure?

A. Yes

B. No

Answer – B

Explanation:

Currently availability zones are not available in all regions. You need to check first on the availability of zones in a region.

Below is the snapshot from the Microsoft documentation

Regions that support Availability Zones

- Central US
- East US 2
- France Central
- North Europe
- Southeast Asia
- West Europe
- West US 2

For more information on availability zones, please visit the below URL

https://docs.microsoft.com/en-us/azure/availability-zones/az-overview

100.   A company is planning on creating resources for different departments in Azure. They want to ensure that they get the bills department wise. Which of the following should you consider implementing for this requirement?

A. Azure locks
B. Azure tags
C. Azure Monitor
D. Azure Advisor

Answer – B

Explanation:

The Microsoft documentation mentions the following

Use tags to organize your Azure resources

11/20/2018 · 10 minutes to read · Contributors

You apply tags to your Azure resources giving metadata to logically organize them into a taxonomy. Each tag consists of a name and a value pair. For example, you can apply the name "Environment" and the value "Production" to all the resources in production.

After you apply tags, you can retrieve all the resources in your subscription with that tag name and value. Tags enable you to retrieve related resources from different resource groups. This approach is helpful when you need to organize resources for billing or management.

An example is given below. Below is a resource being tagged. A department name and value are used as the tag.

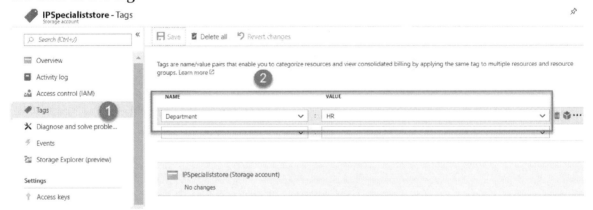

Then in cost analysis, you can segregate costs based on tags

Option A is incorrect since this is used to ensure that resources don't get accidentally deleted

Option C is incorrect since this is used to monitor resources

Option D is incorrect since this is used for providing recommendations in Azure

For more information on using tags, please visit the below URL

https://docs.microsoft.com/en-us/azure/azure-resource-manager/resource-group-using-tags

101. A company needs to create a set of resources in Azure. They have the requirement for IT Administrators that they create resources only in a certain region. Which of the following can help achieve this?

A. Azure Tags
B. Azure Policies
C. Azure Resource Groups
D. Azure Locks

Answer – B

Explanation:

You can use Azure policy for governance of your resources. An example policy on this line is shown below

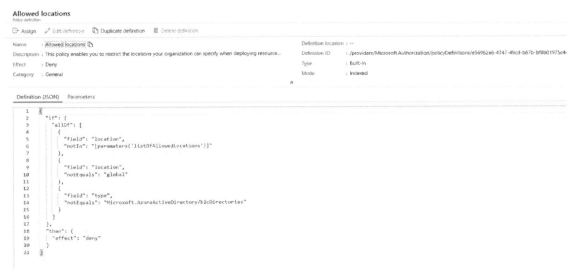

Option A is incorrect since this is used for management and billing purpose

Option C is incorrect since this is used to group resources

Option D is incorrect since this is used to ensure that resources don't get accidentally deleted

For more information on Azure policies, please visit the below URL

https://docs.microsoft.com/en-us/azure/governance/policy/overview

102. Under which of the following cloud computing models would the Azure "Content Delivery" service fall into?

A. Infrastructure as a service (IaaS)

B. Platform as a service (PaaS)

C. Software as a service (SaaS)

D. Function as a service (FaaS)

Answer – B

Explanation:

The Platform for hosting Azure CDN is managed completely by Azure. Below is the description of the service from the Microsoft documentation

What is a content delivery network on Azure?

05/09/2018 · 3 minutes to read · Contributors 🟤🟤🟤🟤🟤 all

A content delivery network (CDN) is a distributed network of servers that can efficiently deliver web content to users. CDNs store cached content on edge servers in point-of-presence (POP) locations that are close to end users, to minimize latency.

Azure Content Delivery Network (CDN) offers developers a global solution for rapidly delivering high-bandwidth content to users by caching their content at strategically placed physical nodes across the world. Azure CDN can also accelerate dynamic content, which cannot be cached, by leveraging various network optimizations using CDN POPs. For example, route optimization to bypass Border Gateway Protocol (BGP).

The benefits of using Azure CDN to deliver web site assets include:

- Better performance and improved user experience for end users, especially when using applications in which multiple round-trips are required to load content.
- Large scaling to better handle instantaneous high loads, such as the start of a product launch event.
- Distribution of user requests and serving of content directly from edge servers so that less traffic is sent to the origin server.

Since this is the right category for the service, all other options are incorrect.

- For more information on the Azure CDN service, please visit the below URL

    o https://docs.microsoft.com/en-us/azure/cdn/cdn-overview

    o https://azure.microsoft.com/en-in/blog/enable-azure-cdn-directly-from-azure-cloud-services-portal-extension/

103.   A company wants to host an application in Azure. The application connects to a database in Azure. The company would like to store the database password in a secure location.

You recommend the usage of the Azure key vault for storage of the password.

Would this fulfill the requirement?

A. Yes

B. No

Answer – A

Explanation:

Yes, this is the right tool to use. Below is what the Microsoft documentation states about this service.

What is Azure Key Vault?

01/18/2019 • 6 minutes to read • Contributors 👤👤👤👤 all

Azure Key Vault helps solve the following problems:

- **Secrets Management** - Azure Key Vault can be used to Securely store and tightly control access to tokens, passwords, certificates, API keys, and other secrets.
- **Key Management** - Azure Key Vault can also be used as a Key Management solution. Azure Key Vault makes it easy to create and control the encryption keys used to encrypt your data.
- **Certificate Management** - Azure Key Vault is also a service that lets you easily provision, manage, and deploy public and private Secure Sockets Layer/Transport Layer Security (SSL/TLS) certificates for use with Azure and your internal connected resources.
- **Store secrets backed by Hardware Security Modules** - The secrets and keys can be protected either by software or FIPS 140-2 Level 2 validates HSMs.

- For more information on the Azure Key vault, please visit the below URL
  - https://docs.microsoft.com/en-us/azure/key-vault/key-vault-whatis

104.   A company wants to host an application in Azure. The application connects to a database in Azure. The company wants to store the database password in a secure location.

You recommend the usage of the Azure Security Center for storage of the password.

A. Yes
B. No

Answer – B

Explanation:

This is used more of a protective layer for your resources in Azure. Below is what the Microsoft documentation states about this service.

What is Azure Security Center?

01/15/2019 • 8 minutes to read • Contributors 👤👤👤👤👤

Azure Security Center is a unified infrastructure security management system that strengthens the security posture of your data centers, and provides advanced threat protection across your hybrid workloads in the cloud - whether they're in Azure or not - as well as on premises.

Keeping your resources safe is a joint effort between your cloud provider, Azure, and you, the customer. You have to make sure your workloads are secure as you move to the cloud, and at the same time, when you move to IaaS (infrastructure as a service) there is more customer responsibility than there was in PaaS (platform as a service), and SaaS (software as a service). Azure Security Center provides you the tools needed to harden your network, secure your services and make sure you're on top of your security posture.

For more information on the Azure Security Service, please visit the below URL
https://docs.microsoft.com/en-us/azure/security-center/security-center-intro

105.   A company wants to host an application in Azure. The application connects to a database in Azure. The company wants to store the database password in a secure location.

You recommend the usage of the Azure Advisor for storage of the password.

Would this fulfill the requirement?

A. Yes
B. No

Answer – B

Explanation:

This is a recommendation tool. Below is what the Microsoft documentation states about this service.

What is Advisor? ☍

Advisor is a personalized cloud consultant that helps you follow best practices to optimize your Azure deployments. It analyzes your resource configuration and usage telemetry and then recommends solutions that can help you improve the cost effectiveness, performance, high availability, and security of your Azure resources.

With Advisor, you can:

- Get proactive, actionable, and personalized best practices recommendations.
- Improve the performance, security, and high availability of your resources, as you identify opportunities to reduce your overall Azure spend.
- Get recommendations with proposed actions inline.

- For more information on the Azure Advisor, please visit the below URL

    o   https://docs.microsoft.com/en-us/azure/advisor/advisor-overview

106.   A company needs to connect their On-premise data center to an Azure Virtual Network using a Site-to-Site connection. Which of the following would you create as part of this implementation?

Virtual network
Quickstart tutorial

 Load Balancer
Learn more

 Application Gateway
Learn more

 Virtual network gateway
Learn more

A. Virtual Network

B. Load Balancer

C. Application Gateway

D. Virtual Private Network Gateway

Answer – D

Explanation:

The Microsoft documentation mentions the following

What is VPN Gateway?

10/19/2018 · 11 minutes to read · Contributors 🌐 🌐 👤 🌐 🌐 all

A VPN gateway is a specific type of virtual network gateway that is used to send encrypted traffic between an Azure virtual network and an on-premises location over the public Internet. You can also use a VPN gateway to send encrypted traffic between Azure virtual networks over the Microsoft network. Each virtual network can have only one VPN gateway. However, you can create multiple connections to the same VPN gateway. When you create multiple connections to the same VPN gateway, all VPN tunnels share the available gateway bandwidth.

Option A is incorrect since this is used to create a network in Azure

Options B and C are incorrect since this is used to divert traffic to backend Virtual Machines

For more information on the Virtual Private gateway, please visit the below URL

- https://docs.microsoft.com/en-us/azure/vpn-gateway/vpn-gateway-about-vpngateways

107. A company is planning on setting up a private cloud network. Which of the following is an advantage of setting up a private cloud network?

A. A Private Cloud environment can only support an Infrastructure as a service model

B. A Private Cloud environment can only support a Platform as a service model

C. The Private Cloud environment can be rolled out to the general public

D. The Private Cloud environment can be rolled out to select users

Answer - D

Explanation:

The Microsoft documentation mentions the following

What is a private cloud?

The private cloud is defined as computing services offered either over the Internet or a private internal network and only to select users instead of the general public. Also called an internal or corporate cloud, private cloud computing gives businesses many of the benefits of a public cloud - including self-service, scalability, and elasticity - with the additional control and customization available from dedicated resources over a computing infrastructure hosted on-premises. In addition, private clouds deliver a higher level of security and privacy through both company firewalls and internal hosting to ensure operations and sensitive data are not accessible to third-party providers. One drawback is that the company's IT department is held responsible for the cost and accountability of managing the private cloud. So private clouds require the same staffing, management, and maintenance expenses as traditional datacenter ownership.

Two models for cloud services can be delivered in a private cloud. The first is infrastructure as a service (IaaS) that allows a company to use infrastructure resources such as compute, network, and storage as a service. The second is platform as a service (PaaS) that lets a company deliver everything from simple cloud-based applications to sophisticated-enabled enterprise applications. Private clouds can also be combined with public clouds to create a hybrid cloud, allowing the business to take advantage of cloud bursting to free up more space and scale computing services to the public cloud when computing demand increases.

Since this is clearly mentioned, all other options are incorrect

For more information on the private cloud network, please visit the below URL

https://azure.microsoft.com/en-us/overview/what-is-a-private-cloud/

108. A company wants to setup resources in Azure. They want a way to manage identities in Azure. Which of the following is used as an Identity Management solution in Azure?

A. Azure AD

B. Azure Advisor

C. Azure Security Center

D. Azure Monitor

Answer – A

Explanation:

The Microsoft documentation mentions the following

What is Azure Active Directory?

11/13/2018 • 9 minutes to read • Contributors 🌑🌑✳️🌑🌑 all

Azure Active Directory (Azure AD) is Microsoft's cloud-based identity and access management service. Azure AD helps your employees sign in and access resources in:

- External resources, such as Microsoft Office 365, the Azure portal, and thousands of other SaaS applications.

- Internal resources, such as apps on your corporate network and intranet, along with any cloud apps developed by your own organization.

Option B is incorrect since this is used to provide recommendations

Option C is incorrect since this is used to protect resources in Azure

Option D is incorrect since this is used to monitor resources in Azure

For more information on Azure AD, please visit the below URL

https://docs.microsoft.com/en-us/azure/active-directory/fundamentals/active-directory-whatis

---

109.   You are planning on setting up an Azure Free account. Which of the following is not correct when it comes to what is offered as part of the Azure Free account?

A. 200 USD free credit to use for 30 days

B. Free access to certain Azure products for 12 months

C. Free access to most popular Azure products after the 12 months' expiration period

D. Access to certain products that are always free

Answer - C

Explanation:

The Microsoft documentation mentions the following

What is the Azure free account?

The Azure free account includes $200 credit to spend for the first 30 days of sign up, free access to our most popular Azure products for 12 months, and access to more than 25 products that are always free.

Since this is clearly mentioned in the Microsoft documentation , all other options are incorrect

For more information on Azure Free account, please visit the below URL

- https://azure.microsoft.com/en-us/free/free-account-faq/

110. Your company is planning on using the Azure App Service (PaaS) to host their set of web applications. Does Azure provide you full control over the operating system that hosts the web applications?

A. Yes

B. No

Answer – B

Explanation:

If you look at the PaaS definition from the Microsoft documentation, you can see that the underlying infrastructure is abstracted away from you and you don't need to manage the infrastructure

Platform as a service (PaaS) is a complete development and deployment environment in the cloud, with resources that enable you to deliver everything from simple cloud-based apps to sophisticated, cloud-enabled enterprise applications. You purchase the resources you need from a cloud service provider on a pay-as-you-go basis and access them over a secure Internet connection.

Like IaaS, PaaS includes infrastructure—servers, storage, and networking—but also middleware, development tools, business intelligence (BI) services, database management systems, and more. PaaS is designed to support the complete web application lifecycle: building, testing, deploying, managing, and updating.

PaaS allows you to avoid the expense and complexity of buying and managing software licenses, the underlying application infrastructure and middleware or the development tools and other resources. You manage the applications and services you develop, and the cloud service provider typically manages everything else.

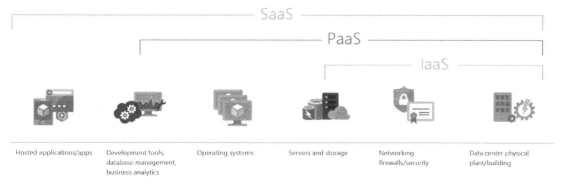

For more information on Platform as a service, please visit the below URL

https://azure.microsoft.com/en-us/overview/what-is-paas/

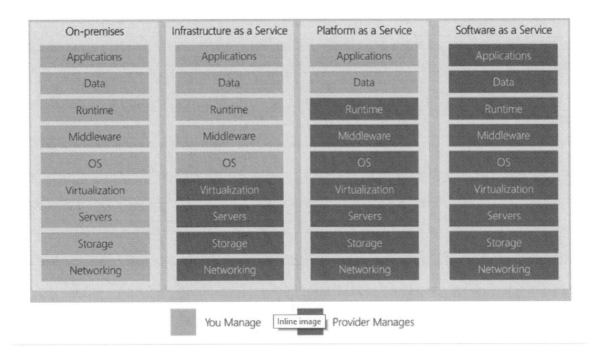

On-premises	Infrastructure as a Service	Platform as a Service	Software as a Service
Applications	Applications	Applications	Applications
Data	Data	Data	Data
Runtime	Runtime	Runtime	Runtime
Middleware	Middleware	Middleware	Middleware
OS	OS	OS	OS
Virtualization	Virtualization	Virtualization	Virtualization
Servers	Servers	Servers	Servers
Storage	Storage	Storage	Storage
Networking	Networking	Networking	Networking

You Manage   Inline image Provider Manages

111. Your company is planning on using the Azure App Service (PaaS) to host their set of web applications. Does Azure provide the ability to scale the platform automatically?

A. Yes

B. No

Answer – A

Explanation:

Azure Web Apps have a lot of ways to scale their infrastructure based on the demand and load on the web app itself.

The Microsoft documentations shows ways in which you can scale up and scale out

- Scale up: Get more CPU, memory, disk space, and extra features like dedicated virtual machines (VMs), custom domains and certificates, staging slots, autoscaling, and more. You scale up by changing the pricing tier of the App Service plan that your app belongs to.
- Scale out: Increase the number of VM instances that run your app. You can scale out to as many as 20 instances, depending on your pricing tier. App Service Environments in **Isolated** tier further increases your scale-out count to 100 instances. For more information about scaling out, see Scale instance count manually or automatically. There, you find out how to use autoscaling, which is to scale instance count automatically based on predefined rules and schedules.

For more information on web app scaling, please visit the below URL

https://docs.microsoft.com/en-us/azure/app-service/web-sites-scale

112. Your company is planning on using the Azure App Service (PaaS) to host their set of web applications. As part of the App Service plan, does Microsoft automatically provide professional services and customizations to applications hosted in Azure Web Apps?

A. Yes
B. No

Answer – B

Explanation:

For any sort of professional services, you have to separately buy the appropriate support plan. It does not come as part of the App service plan

For more information on the support plans, please visit the below URL

https://azure.microsoft.com/en-us/support/plans/

113. A company is planning on hosting their resources in Azure. The senior management wants to know what the capital expenditure (CapEx) and operational expenditure (OpEx) that would be incurred when moving to Azure. Does Azure provide flexibility when it comes to capital expenditure (CapEx) and operational expenditure (OpEx)?

A. Yes
B. No

Answer – A

Explanation:

Azure has many different pricing models for its services.

- You have the Pay-as-you-go model where you only pay for the services you use
- You can use Reserved pricing. An example is the case with Virtual Machines in Azure. You can use Reserved pricing, pay an upfront cost and get huge discounts in the long run.

For more information on pricing for Azure, please visit the below URL

https://azure.microsoft.com/en-us/pricing/

114. A company is planning on setting up a Pay-as-you-go subscription in Azure. Would they have access to MSDN support forums?

A. Yes

B. No

Answer – A

Explanation:

MSDN is a free support plan and has no linkage with the subscription

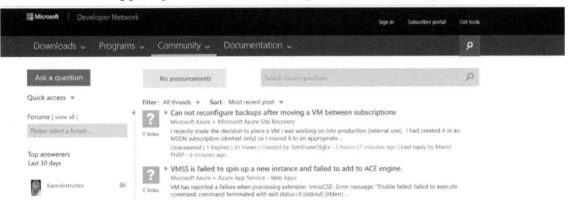

For more information on MSDN forums, please visit the below URL

https://social.msdn.microsoft.com/forums/en-us/home

115. A company wants to migrate their current on-premise servers to Azure. They want to ensure that the servers are running even if a single Azure Data Center goes down. Which of the following terms refers to the solution that needs to be in place to fulfil this requirement?

A. Fault tolerance

B. Elasticity

C. Scalability

D. Low Latency

Answer – A

Explanation:

This concept of Fault tolerance refers to achieving high availability on the cloud.

Options B and C are incorrect since this refers to how best you can scale up or down based on demand

Option D is incorrect since this refers to data transfer

For more information on resiliency in Azure, please visit the below URL

https://azure.microsoft.com/en-us/features/resiliency/

116. When can an organization completely decommission their on-premise data center?

A. When they have a hybrid solution

B. When all of their servers are in the private cloud

C. When all of their servers are in the public cloud

D. When all of their servers are in the public or private cloud

Answer – D

Explanation:

When all the servers are migrated to the Azure cloud which can be Public / Private and you have no dependency left on your on-premise environment, then you can completely look to decommission your on-premise data center.

For more information on migration tools available for Azure, please visit the below URL

https://azure.microsoft.com/en-us/migration/

117. A company is planning on migrating their public web site to Azure. Which of the following do they need to consider when it comes to hosting their public web site on Azure?

A. They would need to reduce the number of connections to the web site

B. They would need to deploy a Virtual Private connection from their on-premise site to Azure

C. They would have to consider paying a monthly cost for the solution

D. They would need to pay for the user data transfer onto the site

Answer – C

Explanation:

If you need to host a web application in Azure, there are a couple of options. But for each option, you have to pay a monthly fee. An example is the pricing model available for Azure Web apps. If you are planning on deploying a public web site, then you would need to consider using a Basic App service plan or higher.

	FREE Try for free	SHARED Environment for dev/test	BASIC Dedicated environment for dev/test	STANDARD Run production workloads	PREMIUM Enhanced performance and scale	ISOLATED High-Performance, Security and Isolation
Web, mobile, or API apps	10	100	Unlimited	Unlimited	Unlimited	Unlimited
Disk space	1 GB	1 GB	10 GB	50 GB	250 GB	1 TB
Maximum instances	–	–	Up to 3	Up to 10	Up to 20	Up to 100*
Custom domain	–	Supported	Supported	Supported	Supported	Supported
Auto Scale	–	–	–	Supported	Supported	Supported
VPN hybrid connectivity	–	–	–	Supported	Supported	Supported
Network Isolation						Supported
Price per hour	Free	$0.013	$0.075	$0.10	$0.20	$0.30

- Option A is incorrect because Azure can support a high number of connections
- Option B is incorrect since only if you need to connect your web application to a resource in your on-premise data center then maybe you need to consider this.
- Option D is incorrect since you don't need to pay for the data transfer
- For more information on Azure App service plans, please visit the below URL
    o https://azure.microsoft.com/en-us/pricing/details/app-service/windows/

118. A company needs the list of planned maintenance events that can affect the availability of an Azure subscription. Which of the following would help them achieve this requirement?

A. App Services

B. Resource Groups

C. Virtual Machines

D. Azure Active Directory

E. Security Center

F. Cost Management + Billing

G. Help + Support

Answer – G

Explanation:

If you go to Help + Support and then go to Service Health, then you can view if there are any issues to the underlying Azure Infrastructure.

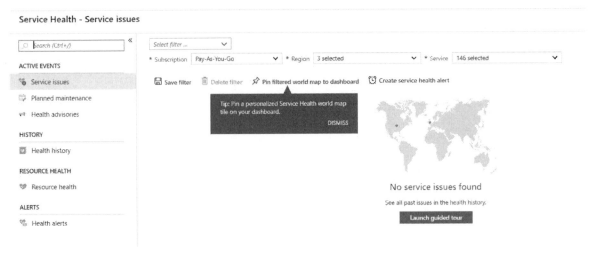

Service Health - Service issues

The other services will not give you this view.

For more information on Azure service health, please visit the below URL

- https://azure.microsoft.com/en-us/features/service-health/

Ask our Experts

119. A company has several on-premise computers that run Windows 10. They want to map a network drive from these machines onto Azure Storage. Which of the following would you consider fulfilling this requirement?

A. An Azure SQL Database

B. An Azure SQL Datawarehouse

C. Azure Storage account – BLOB service

D. Azure Storage account – File service

Answer – D

Explanation:

Below is an example of this

1. Here we have a storage account using the File service
2. A file share named demo is defined. If you click on the Connect button for the file share
3. You will get the instructions to map a drive to the file share

None of the other solutions have the facility to map network drives.

For more information on Azure File shares, please visit the below URL

https://docs.microsoft.com/en-us/azure/storage/files/storage-files-planning

120.   A company has a VPN device that will be used on a Site-to-Site connection from an on-premise location to Azure. Which of the following would be used to represent the VPN device?

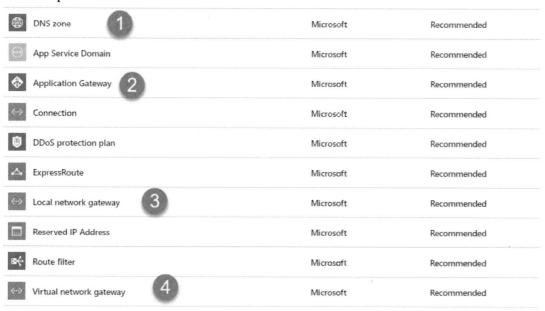

A. DNS Zone

B. Application gateway

C. Local network gateway

D. Virtual Network gateway

Answer – C

Explanation:

This is clearly given in the Microsoft documentation

5. Create the local network gateway

The local network gateway typically refers to your on-premises location. You give the site a name by which Azure can refer to it, then specify the IP address of the on-premises VPN device to which you will create a connection. You also specify the IP address prefixes that will be routed through the VPN gateway to the VPN device. The address prefixes you specify are the prefixes located on your on-premises network. If your on-premises network changes or you need to change the public IP address for the VPN device, you can easily update the values later.

Since this is clearly given, all other options are incorrect

For more information on creating a site to site connection, please visit the below URL

https://docs.microsoft.com/en-us/azure/vpn-gateway/vpn-gateway-howto-site-to-site-resource-manager-portal

121. A company wants to deploy an Artificial Intelligence solution in Azure. The development team wants to have a tool in place that can be used to build, test, and deploy predictive analytics solutions. Which of the following should they use for this purpose?

A. Azure Logic Apps

B. Azure Machine Learning Studio

C. Azure Batch

D. Azure App service

Answer – B

Explanation:

The Microsoft documentation mentions the following on Azure Machine Learning Studio

What is Azure Machine Learning Studio?

03/28/2018 · 9 minutes to read · Contributors 🔵🔵🔵🔵🔵

Microsoft Azure Machine Learning Studio is a collaborative, drag-and-drop tool you can use to build, test, and deploy predictive analytics solutions on your data. Machine Learning Studio publishes models as web services that can easily be consumed by custom apps or BI tools such as Excel.

Machine Learning Studio is where data science, predictive analytics, cloud resources, and your data meet.

Option A is incorrect since this is used to define workflows in Azure

Option C is incorrect since this is used for batch processing applications

Option D is incorrect since this is used to host Apps in Azure such as Web based applications

For more information on Azure Machine Learning Studio, please visit the below URL

https://docs.microsoft.com/en-us/azure/machine-learning/studio/what-is-ml-studio

122.	A company has a set of resources deployed to Azure. They want to make use of the Azure Advisor tool. Would the Azure Advisor tool give recommendations on how to reduce the cost of running Azure Virtual Machines?

A. Yes

B. No

Answer – A

Explanation:

Yes, it does, below is an example of this. Below is a recommendation being given to purchase reserved instances to save on costs.

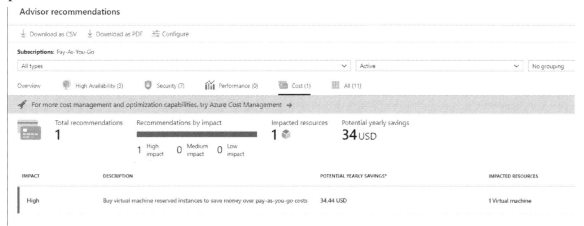

For more information on Azure Advisor cost recommendations, please visit the below URL

https://docs.microsoft.com/en-us/azure/advisor/advisor-cost-recommendations

123.   A company has a set of IT engineers that are responsible for implementing and managing the resources in their Azure account. The IT engineers have a set of on-premise workstations that have the following flavors of operating systems

- Windows 10
- MacOS
- Ubuntu

Which of the following tools can you use on the Windows 10 machines?

A. The Azure CLI and Azure Portal only

B. The Azure CLI and Powershell only

C. The Azure Portal and Powershell only

D. The Azure CLI, Azure Powershell and Azure Portal

Answer – D

Explanation:

The Azure portal can be viewed on any browser and hence can be viewed on almost all operating systems

The Azure CLI is available on all platforms as shown below in the Microsoft documentation

Install the Azure CLI

11/16/2018 · 2 minutes to read · Contributors 🧑 👤 👤 👤 ⊗ all

The Azure CLI is a command-line tool providing a great experience for managing Azure resources. The CLI is designed to make scripting easy, query data, support long-running operations, and more. Try it today and find out what the CLI has to offer!

The current version of the CLI is **2.0.57**. For information about the latest release, see the release notes.

- Install on Windows
- Install on macOS
- Install on Linux or Windows Subsystem for Linux (WSL)
  - Install with apt on Debian or Ubuntu
  - Install with yum on RHEL, Fedora, or CentOS
  - Install with zypper on openSUSE or SLE
  - Install from script
- Run in Docker container

Azure Powershell is available on all platforms as shown below in the Microsoft documentation

Install the Azure PowerShell module

12/13/2018 · 3 minutes to read · Contributors 🧑 👤

This article tells you how to install the Azure PowerShell modules using PowerShellGet. These instructions work on Windows, macOS, and Linux platforms. For the Az module, currently no other installation methods are supported.

- For more information on Azure CLI and Azure powershell, please visit the below URL
  - https://docs.microsoft.com/en-us/cli/azure/install-azure-cli?view=azure-cli-latest
  - https://docs.microsoft.com/en-us/powershell/azure/install-az-ps?view=azps-1.2.0

124.   A company has a set of IT engineers that are responsible for implementing and managing the resources in their Azure account. The IT engineers have a set of on-premise workstations that have the following favors of operating systems

- Windows 10
- MacOS
- Ubuntu

Which of the following tools can you use on the Ubuntu machines?

A. The Azure CLI and Azure Portal only

B. The Azure CLI and Powershell only

C. The Azure Portal and Powershell only

D. The Azure CLI, Azure Powershell, and Azure Portal

Answer – D

Explanation:

The Azure portal can be viewed on any browser and hence can be viewed on almost all operating systems

The Azure CLI is available on all platforms as shown below in the Microsoft documentation

Install the Azure CLI

11/16/2018 • 2 minutes to read • Contributors 🔵 🔵 🔵 🔵 🔵 all

The Azure CLI is a command-line tool providing a great experience for managing Azure resources. The CLI is designed to make scripting easy, query data, support long-running operations, and more. Try it today and find out what the CLI has to offer!

The current version of the CLI is **2.0.57**. For information about the latest release, see the release notes.

- Install on Windows
- Install on macOS
- Install on Linux or Windows Subsystem for Linux (WSL)
  - Install with apt on Debian or Ubuntu
  - Install with yum on RHEL, Fedora, or CentOS
  - Install with zypper on openSUSE or SLE
  - Install from script
- Run in Docker container

Azure Powershell is available on all platforms as shown below in the Microsoft documentation

Install the Azure PowerShell module

12/13/2018 • 3 minutes to read • Contributors 🔵 🔵

This article tells you how to install the Azure PowerShell modules using PowerShellGet. These instructions work on Windows, macOS, and Linux platforms. For the Az module, currently no other installation methods are supported.

For more information on Azure CLI and Azure Powershell, please visit the below URL

https://docs.microsoft.com/en-us/cli/azure/install-azure-cli?view=azure-cli-latest

https://docs.microsoft.com/en-us/powershell/azure/install-az-ps?view=azps-1.2.0

125. A company has a set of IT engineers that are responsible for implementing and manging the resources in their Azure account. The IT engineers have a set of on-premise workstations that have the following favours of operating systems

- Windows 10
- MacOS

- Ubuntu

Which of the following tools can you use on the MacOS machines?

    A. The Azure CLI and Azure Portal only

    B. The Azure CLI and Powershell only

    C. The Azure Portal and Powershell only

    D. The Azure CLI, Azure Powershell and Azure Portal

Answer – D

Explanation:

The Azure portal can be viewed on any browser and hence can be viewed on almost all operating systems

The Azure CLI is available on all platforms as shown below in the Microsoft documentation

Install the Azure CLI

11/16/2018 · 2 minutes to read · Contributors 👤 ⚫ ⚫ ⚫ ⚫ all

The Azure CLI is a command-line tool providing a great experience for managing Azure resources. The CLI is designed to make scripting easy, query data, support long-running operations, and more. Try it today and find out what the CLI has to offer!

The current version of the CLI is **2.0.57**. For information about the latest release, see the release notes.

- Install on Windows
- Install on macOS
- Install on Linux or Windows Subsystem for Linux (WSL)
  - Install with apt on Debian or Ubuntu
  - Install with yum on RHEL, Fedora, or CentOS
  - Install with zypper on openSUSE or SLE
  - Install from script
- Run in Docker container

Azure Powershell is available on all platforms as shown below in the Microsoft documentation

Install the Azure PowerShell module

12/13/2018 · 3 minutes to read · Contributors 👤 👤

This article tells you how to install the Azure PowerShell modules using PowerShellGet. These instructions work on Windows, macOS, and Linux platforms. For the Az module, currently no other installation methods are supported.

For more information on Azure CLI and Azure powershell, please visit the below URL

https://docs.microsoft.com/en-us/cli/azure/install-azure-cli?view=azure-cli-latest

https://docs.microsoft.com/en-us/powershell/azure/install-az-ps?view=azps-1.2.0

126.   A company is planning on setting up a solution in Azure. The solution would have the following key requirement

- Provides a platform for creating workflows

Which of the following would be best suited for this requirement?

    A. Azure Databricks

    B. Azure Logic Apps

    C. Azure App Service

    D. Azure Application Insights

Answer – B

Explanation:

The Microsoft documentation mentions the following

What is Azure Logic Apps?

06/29/2018 · 8 minutes to read · Contributors ● ● ⚙

Azure Logic Apps is a cloud service that helps you automate and orchestrate tasks, business processes, and workflows when you need to integrate apps, data, systems, and services across enterprises or organizations. Logic Apps simplifies how you design and build scalable solutions for app integration, data integration, system integration, enterprise application integration (EAI), and business-to-business (B2B) communication, whether in the cloud, on premises, or both.

Since this is a clear feature on the tool, all other options are incorrect

For more information on Azure Logic Apps, please visit the below URL

https://docs.microsoft.com/en-us/azure/logic-apps/logic-apps-overview

127.   A company is planning on setting up a solution in Azure. The solution would have the following key requirement

- Gives the ability to host a big data analysis service for machine learning

Which of the following would be best suited for this requirement?

    A. Azure Databricks

    B. Azure Logic Apps

    C. Azure App Service

    D. Azure Application Insights

Answer – A

Explanation:

The Microsoft documentation mentions the following

What is Azure Databricks?

05/29/2018 · 3 minutes to read · Contributors 🔵 🟢 ⚫ 🔵

Azure Databricks is an Apache Spark-based analytics platform optimized for the Microsoft Azure cloud services platform. Designed with the founders of Apache Spark, Databricks is integrated with Azure to provide one-click setup, streamlined workflows, and an interactive workspace that enables collaboration between data scientists, data engineers, and business analysts.

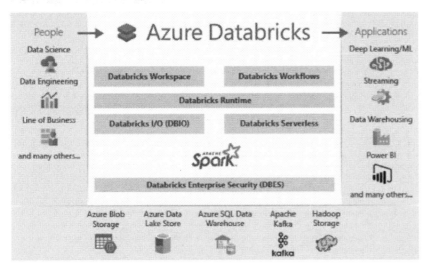

Since this is a clear feature on the tool, all other options are incorrect

For more information on Azure Databricks, please visit the below URL

https://docs.microsoft.com/en-us/azure/azure-databricks/what-is-azure-databricks

128.   A company is planning on setting up a solution in Azure. The solution would have the following key requirement

* Give the ability to detect and diagnose anomalies in web apps

Which of the following would be best suited for this requirement?

    A. Azure Databricks

    B. Azure Logic Apps

    C. Azure App Service

    D. Azure Application Insights

Answer – D

Explanation:

The Microsoft documentation mentions the following

What is Application Insights?

01/23/2019 • 5 minutes to read • Contributors 🌑 🌑 🌑

Application Insights is an extensible Application Performance Management (APM) service for web developers on multiple platforms. Use it to monitor your live web application. It will automatically detect performance anomalies. It includes powerful analytics tools to help you diagnose issues and to understand what users actually do with your app. It's designed to help you continuously improve performance and usability. It works for apps on a wide variety of platforms including .NET, Node.js and J2EE, hosted on-premises, hybrid, or any public cloud. It integrates with your DevOps process, and has connection points to a variety of development tools. It can monitor and analyze telemetry from mobile apps by integrating with Visual Studio App Center.

Since this is a clear feature on the tool, all other options are incorrect

For more information on Azure Application Insights, please visit the below URL

https://docs.microsoft.com/en-us/azure/azure-monitor/app/app-insights-overview

129.   A company is planning on setting up a solution in Azure. The solution would have the following key requirement

- Allows the hosting of web-based applications

Which of the following would be best suited for this requirement?

A. Azure Databricks

B. Azure Logic Apps

C. Azure App Service

D. Azure Application Insights

Answer – C

Explanation:

The Microsoft documentation mentions the following

App Service Documentation

Azure App Service enables you to build and host web apps, mobile back ends, and RESTful APIs in the programming language of your choice without managing infrastructure. It offers auto-scaling and high availability, supports both Windows and Linux, and enables automated deployments from GitHub, Azure DevOps, or any Git repo. Learn how to use Azure App Service with our quickstarts, tutorials, and samples.

Since this is a clear feature on the tool, all other options are incorrect

For more information on Azure App Service, please visit the below URL

https://docs.microsoft.com/en-us/azure/app-service/

130.   A company wants to host an application on a set of Virtual Machines. The application must be made available 99.99 percent of the time.

In order to comply with the SLA requirement, what is the minimum number of Virtual Machines that should be used to host the application?

A. 1

B. 2

C. 3

D. 4

Answer – B

Explanation:

The application should be designed in the following way

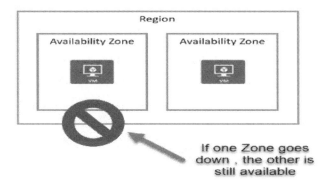

Here you have 2 availability zones and a virtual machine per available zone. If one zone goes down, you still have the other zone available. This is the minimum configuration.

For more information on Availability zones, please visit the below URL

https://docs.microsoft.com/en-us/azure/availability-zones/az-overview

131. A company wants to host an application on a set of Virtual Machines. The application must be made available 99.99 percent of the time.

In order to comply with the SLA requirement, what is the minimum number of availability zones that should be used to host the application?

A. 1

B. 2

C. 3

D. 4

Answer – B

Explanation:

The application should be designed in the following way

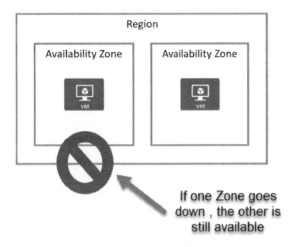

Here you have 2 availability zones and a virtual machine per available zone. If one zone goes down, you still have the other zone available. This is the minimum configuration.

For more information on Availability zones, please visit the below URL

https://docs.microsoft.com/en-us/azure/availability-zones/az-overview

132.   A company is planning on hosting solutions on the Azure Cloud. They need to implement MFA for identities hosted in Azure. There are only two valid ways of authentications for MFA as listed below:

- Picture Identification
- Passport Number

A. True
B. False

Answer – B

Explanation:

The Microsoft documentation mentions the different authentication methods available

What are authentication methods?

01/31/2018 • 9 minutes to read • Contributors 🔵🔵🔵🔵

Azure AD self-service password reset (SSPR) and Multi-Factor Authentication (MFA) may ask for additional information, known as authentication methods or security info, to confirm you are who you say you are when using the associated features.

Administrators can define in policy which authentication methods are available to users of SSPR and MFA. Some authentication methods may not be available to all features.

Microsoft highly recommends Administrators enable users to select more than the minimum required number of authentication methods in case they do not have access to one.

Authentication Method	Usage
Password	MFA and SSPR
Security questions	SSPR Only
Email address	SSPR Only
Microsoft Authenticator app	MFA and public preview for SSPR
OATH Hardware token	Public preview for MFA and SSPR
SMS	MFA and SSPR
Voice call	MFA and SSPR
App passwords	MFA only in certain cases

For more information on the authentication methods, please visit the below URL

- https://docs.microsoft.com/en-us/azure/active-directory/authentication/concept-authentication-methods

133. You are working on understanding all the key terms when it comes to International standards, data privacy and data protection policies.

Which of the following options is related to the statement given below?

"An organization that defines international standards across all industries"

A. Azure Government
B. GDPR
C. ISO
D. NIST

Answer – C

Explanation:

Below is the definition as per Wikipedia

The International Organization for Standardization is an independent, non-governmental organization, the members of which are the standards organizations of the 164[1] member countries. It is the world's largest developer of voluntary international standards and facilitates world trade by providing common standards between nations. Over twenty thousand standards have been set covering everything from manufactured products and technology to food safety, agriculture and healthcare.[3]

Use of the standards aids in the creation of products and services that are safe, reliable and of good quality. The standards help businesses increase productivity while minimizing errors and waste. By enabling products from different markets to be directly compared, they facilitate companies in entering new markets and assist in the development of global trade on a fair basis. The standards also serve to safeguard consumers and the end-users of products and services, ensuring that certified products conform to the minimum standards set internationally.[3]

Since this is clearly mentioned, all other options are incorrect

For more information on ISO, please visit the below URL

https://en.wikipedia.org/wiki/International_Organization_for_Standardization

134.   You are working on understanding all the key terms when it comes to International standards, data privacy and data protection policies.

Which of the following options is related to the statement given below?

"An organization that defines standards used by the United States government"

   A. Azure Government

   B. GDPR

   C. ISO

   D. NIST

Answer – D

Explanation:

The Microsoft documentation gives an overview of the NIST CSF overview

NIST CSF Overview

The National Institute of Standards and Technology (NIST) promotes and maintains measurement standards and guidance to help organizations assess risk. In response to Executive Order 13636 on strengthening the cybersecurity of federal networks and critical infrastructure, NIST released the Framework for Improving Critical Infrastructure Cybersecurity (FICIC) in February 2014.

The main priorities of the FICIC were to establish a set of standards and practices to help organizations manage cybersecurity risk, while enabling business efficiency. The NIST framework addresses cybersecurity risk without imposing additional regulatory requirements for both government and private sector organizations.

The FICIC references globally-recognized standards including NIST SP 800-53 found in Appendix A of the NIST's 2014 Framework for Improving Critical Infrastructure Cybersecurity. Each control within the FICIC framework is mapped to corresponding NIST 800-53 controls within the FedRAMP Moderate Baseline.

For more information on the NIST adoption in Azure, please visit the below URL

https://www.microsoft.com/en-us/trustcenter/compliance/NIST_CSF

135.   You are working on understanding all the key terms when it comes to International standards, data privacy and data protection policies.

Which of the following options is related to the statement given below?

"A European policy that regulates data privacy and data protection"

   A. Azure Government

B. GDPR

C. ISO

D. NIST

Answer – B

Explanation:

Below is the definition as per Wikipedia

The **General Data Protection Regulation** (EU) 2016/679 ("GDPR") is a regulation in EU law on data protection and privacy for all individuals within the European Union (EU) and the European Economic Area (EEA). It also addresses the export of personal data outside the EU and EEA areas. The GDPR aims primarily to give control to individuals over their personal data and to simplify the regulatory environment for international business by unifying the regulation within the EU.[1] Superseding the Data Protection Directive 95/46/EC, the regulation contains provisions and requirements pertaining to the processing of personal data of individuals (formally called *data subjects* in the GDPR) inside the EEA, and applies to an enterprise established in the EEA or—regardless of its location and the data subjects' citizenship—that is processing the personal information of data subjects inside the EEA.

Since this is clearly mentioned, all other options are incorrect

For more information on GPDR, please visit the below URL

https://en.wikipedia.org/wiki/General_Data_Protection_Regulation

136.   You are working on understanding all the key terms when it comes to International standards, data privacy and data protection policies.

Which of the following options is related to the statement given below?

"A dedicated public cloud for federal and state agencies in the United States"

A. Azure Government

B. GDPR

C. ISO

D. NIST

Answer – A

Explanation:

The Microsoft documentation mentions the following

US government agencies or their partners interested in cloud services that meet government security and compliance requirements, can be confident that Microsoft Azure Government provides world-class security, protection, and compliance services. Azure Government delivers a dedicated cloud enabling government agencies and their partners to transform mission-critical workloads to the cloud. Azure Government services handle data that is subject to certain government regulations and requirements, such as FedRAMP, NIST 800.171 (DIB), ITAR, IRS 1075, DoD L4, and CJIS. In order to provide you with the highest level of security and compliance, Azure Government uses physically isolated datacenters and networks (located in U.S. only).

Since this is clearly mentioned in the Microsoft documentation, all other options are invalid

For more information on Azure government, please visit the below URL

https://docs.microsoft.com/en-us/azure/azure-government/documentation-government-welcome

137. A company plans to purchase an Azure Support plan. Below is a key requirement for the support plan

- Provide an option to contact Microsoft support engineers by phone or email

A recommendation is made to purchase the Basic Support plan

Would this recommendation fulfil the requirement?

A. Yes

B. No

Answer – B

Explanation:

As per the Basic Support plan as shown below, this plan has no access to support engineers

	BASIC	DEVELOPER	STANDARD	PROFESSIONAL DIRECT	PREMIER
		Purchase support	Purchase support	Purchase support	Contact Premier
	Azure Advisor recommendations	Azure Advisor recommendations	Azure Advisor recommendations	Azure Advisor recommendations	Azure Advisor recommendations
Health Status and Notifications	Access to personalized Service Health Dashboard & Health API	Access to personalized Service Health Dashboard & Health API	Access to personalized Service Health Dashboard & Health API	Access to personalized Service Health Dashboard & Health API	Access to personalized Service Health Dashboard & Health API
Technical Support		Business hours access[1] to Support Engineers via email	24x7 access to Support Engineers via email and phone	24x7 access to Support Engineers via email and phone	24x7 access to Support Engineers via email and phone

For more information on the support plans, please visit the below URL

https://azure.microsoft.com/en-us/support/plans/

138. A company plans to purchase an Azure Support plan. Below is a key requirement for the support plan

- Provide an option to contact Microsoft support engineers by phone or email

A recommendation is made to purchase the Standard Support plan

Would this recommendation fulfil the requirement?

A. Yes

B. No

Answer – A

Explanation:

Yes, as per the documentation, the plan does have access to support engineers via phone and email

	BASIC	DEVELOPER	STANDARD	PROFESSIONAL DIRECT	PREMIER
		Purchase support	Purchase support	Purchase support	Contact Premier
	Azure Advisor recommendations	Azure Advisor recommendations	Azure Advisor recommendations	Azure Advisor recommendations	Azure Advisor recommendations
Health Status and Notifications	Access to personalized Service Health Dashboard & Health API	Access to personalized Service Health Dashboard & Health API	Access to personalized Service Health Dashboard & Health API	Access to personalized Service Health Dashboard & Health API	Access to personalized Service Health Dashboard & Health API
Technical Support		Business hours access to Support Engineers via email	24x7 access to Support Engineers via email and phone	24x7 access to Support Engineers via email and phone	24x7 access to Support Engineers via email and phone

For more information on the support plans, please visit the below URL

https://azure.microsoft.com/en-us/support/plans/

139.   A company plans to purchase an Azure Support plan. Below is a key requirement for the support plan

- Provide an option to contact Microsoft support engineers by phone or email

A recommendation is made to purchase the Premier Support plan

Would this recommendation fulfil the requirement?

A. Yes
B. No

Answer – A

Explanation:

Yes, as per the documentation, the plan does have access to support engineers via phone and email

	BASIC	DEVELOPER	STANDARD	PROFESSIONAL DIRECT	PREMIER
		Purchase support	Purchase support	Purchase support	Contact Premier
	Azure Advisor recommendations	Azure Advisor recommendations	Azure Advisor recommendations	Azure Advisor recommendations	Azure Advisor recommendations
Health Status and Notifications	Access to personalized Service Health Dashboard & Health API	Access to personalized Service Health Dashboard & Health API	Access to personalized Service Health Dashboard & Health API	Access to personalized Service Health Dashboard & Health API	Access to personalized Service Health Dashboard & Health API
Technical Support		Business hours access[1] to Support Engineers via email	24x7 access to Support Engineers via email and phone	24x7 access to Support Engineers via email and phone	24x7 access to Support Engineers via email and phone

For more information on the support plans, please visit the below URL

https://azure.microsoft.com/en-us/support/plans/

140.   A company is currently planning on deploying resources to Azure. They want to have the ability to manage the user access to resources across multiple subscriptions. Which of the following can help you achieve this requirement?

A. Resource Groups
B. Management Groups
C. Azure Policies
D. Azure App Service

Answer – B

Explanation:

The correct answer is B, Management Groups. From the Microsoft Documentation: Azure Management Groups are containers for managing access across multiple Azure subscriptions.

Another scenario where you would use management groups is to provide user access to multi subscriptions. By moving many subscriptions under that management group, you can create one role-based access control (RBAC) assignment on the management group, which will inherit that access to all the subscriptions. One assignment on the management group can enable users to have access to everything they need instead of scripting RBAC over different subscriptions.

Important facts about management groups

- 10,000 management groups can be supported in a single directory.
- A management group tree can support up to six levels of depth.
  - This limit doesn't include the Root level or the subscription level.
- Each management group and subscription can only support one parent.
- Each management group can have many children.
- All subscriptions and management groups are within a single hierarchy in each directory. See Important facts about the Root management group for exceptions during the Preview.

- Option A is invalid because this is good for grouping your resources together.
- Option C is incorect because Azure Policies are valid only within one subscription.
- Option D is invalid because this is used to host your web applications.

For more information on Management Groups, please visit the below URL

- https://docs.microsoft.com/en-us/azure/governance/management-groups/

For more information on Azure policies, please visit the below URL

- https://docs.microsoft.com/en-us/azure/governance/policy/overview

141. Most Azure services normally follow the below lifecycle

- First they are deployed in private preview
- Then are released in public preview
- And then finally they are released in General availability

Is this true for the lifecycle for an Azure service?

    A. Yes

    B. No

Answer – A

Explanation:

This is generally the case for new products on the Azure platform.

So, first Azure allows customers to try out products in the private preview. For the product the customer would fill up a form. And then Microsoft would make the product available for preview for just the customer.

Next the service would be available in public preview based on a select criterion.

And then finally the service would be available to the general public.

For more information on updates to the Azure platform, please visit the below URL

https://azure.microsoft.com/en-us/updates

142.   A company wants to try out a couple of Azure services which are available in public preview. Is it true that services in public preview can only be used via the Azure command line interface?

    A. Yes

    B. No

Answer – B

Explanation:

This is not necessarily true. An example is given below. Here there is a preview available for Virtual Machines in Azure Monitor.

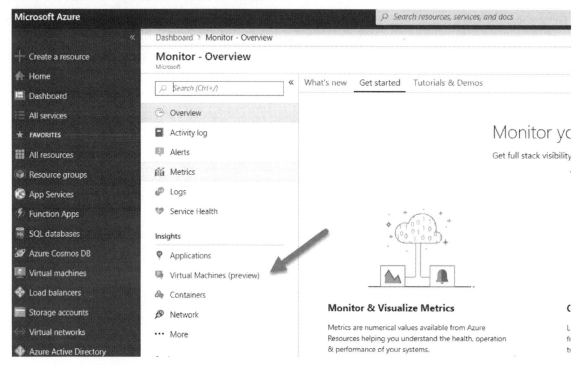

For more information on updates to the Azure platform, please visit the below URL

https://azure.microsoft.com/en-us/updates

143.   A company is planning on setting up an Azure account and spinning up resources in the purchased subscription. When it comes to the Service Level Agreement, does Microsoft provide an SLA of 99.99% uptime for Storage Accounts?

A. Yes

B. No

Answer – A

Explanation:

Storage Accounts

- We guarantee that at least 99.99% (99.9% for Cool Access Tier) of the time, we will successfully process requests to read data from Read Access-Geo Redundant Storage (RA-GRS) Accounts, provided that failed attempts to read data from the primary region are retried on the secondary region.

- We guarantee that at least 99.9% (99% for Cool Access Tier) of the time, we will successfully process requests to read data from Locally Redundant Storage (LRS), Zone Redundant Storage (ZRS), and Geo Redundant Storage (GRS) Accounts.

- We guarantee that at least 99.9% (99% for Cool Access Tier) of the time, we will successfully process requests to write data to Locally Redundant Storage (LRS), Zone Redundant Storage (ZRS), and Geo Redundant Storage (GRS) Accounts and Read Access-Geo Redundant Storage (RA-GRS) Accounts.

If you view the Summary of SLA's in the below given link, you will see most of the services do give a 99.99% SLA.

https://azure.microsoft.com/en-us/support/legal/sla/summary/

144.   A company is planning on setting up a solution in Azure. They need to host a web application. Which of the following is best suited for this requirement? Please select 2 options.

A. Azure Data Lake Analytics

B. Azure Virtual Machine scale sets

C. Azure Kubernetes

D. Azure App Service

Answer – C and D

Explanation:

You can use Azure Kubernetes for the managing container-based solutions.

The Microsoft documentation mentions the following

Ship faster, operate with ease, and scale confidently	The fully managed Azure Kubernetes Service (AKS) makes deploying and managing containerized applications easy. It offers serverless Kubernetes, an integrated continuous integration and continuous delivery (CI/CD) experience, and enterprise-grade security and governance. Unite your development and operations teams on a single platform to rapidly build, deliver, and scale applications with confidence.

Option A is incorrect since this is used for Big Data solutions

Option B is incorrect since this is used for scaling virtual machines

Option D is correct since this is used for hosting web applications in Azure

For more information on Azure Kubernetes, please visit the following URL

https://azure.microsoft.com/en-us/services/kubernetes-service/

145.   A company is planning on setting up a solution in Azure. The solution would have the following key requirement

• Provide a solution to create and manage a group of identical, load balanced Virtual Machines.

Which of the following would be best suited for this requirement?

A. Azure Data Lake Analytics

B. Azure Virtual Machine Scale Sets

C. Azure Virtual Network

D. Azure App Service

Answer – B

Explanation:

The Microsoft documentation mentions the following

What are virtual machine scale sets?

03/27/2018 · 3 minutes to read · Contributors ● ● ●

Azure virtual machine scale sets let you create and manage a group of identical, load balanced VMs. The number of VM instances can automatically increase or decrease in response to demand or a defined schedule. Scale sets provide high availability to your applications, and allow you to centrally manage, configure, and update a large number of VMs. With virtual machine scale sets, you can build large-scale services for areas such as compute, big data, and container workloads.

Since this is a clear feature on the tool, all other options are incorrect

For more information on Azure Virtual Machine Scale sets, please visit the below URL

https://docs.microsoft.com/en-us/azure/virtual-machine-scale-sets/overview

146.   A company is planning on setting up a solution in Azure. The solution would have the following key requirement

- Provide an isolated environment for hosting of Virtual Machines

Which of the following would be best suited for this requirement?

   A. Azure Data Lake Analytics

   B. Azure Virtual Machine Scale Sets

   C. Azure Virtual Network

   D. Azure App Service

Answer – C

Explanation:

The Microsoft documentation mentions the following

What is Azure Virtual Network?

12/12/2018 • 4 minutes to read • Contributors ●●●●● all

Azure Virtual Network enables many types of Azure resources, such as Azure Virtual Machines (VM), to securely communicate with each other, the internet, and on-premises networks. A virtual network is scoped to a single region; however, multiple virtual networks from different regions can be connected together using Virtual Network Peering.

Azure Virtual Network provides the following key capabilities:

Isolation and segmentation

You can implement multiple virtual networks within each Azure subscription and Azure region. Each virtual network is isolated from other virtual networks. For each virtual network you can:

- Specify a custom private IP address space using public and private (RFC 1918) addresses. Azure assigns resources in a virtual network a private IP address from the address space that you assign.
- Segment the virtual network into one or more subnets and allocate a portion of the virtual network's address space to each subnet.
- Use Azure-provided name resolution, or specify your own DNS server, for use by resources in a virtual network.

Since this is a clear feature on the tool, all other options are incorrect

For more information on Azure Virtual Network, please visit the below URL

https://docs.microsoft.com/en-us/azure/virtual-network/virtual-networks-overview

147.   A company is planning on setting up a solution in Azure. The solution would have the following key requirement

- Provide a cloud service that helps to transform data and provide valuable insights on the data itself

Which of the following would be best suited for this requirement?

A. Azure Data Lake Analytics

B. Azure Virtual Machine Scale Sets

C. Azure Virtual Network

D. Azure App Service

Answer – A

Explanation:

The Microsoft documentation mentions the following

What is Azure Data Lake Analytics?

06/23/2017 · 2 minutes to read · Contributors 🌑🌑🌑🌑 all

Azure Data Lake Analytics is an on-demand analytics job service that simplifies big data. Instead of deploying, configuring, and tuning hardware, you write queries to transform your data and extract valuable insights. The analytics service can handle jobs of any scale instantly by setting the dial for how much power you need. You only pay for your job when it is running, making it cost-effective.

Since this is a clear feature on the tool, all other options are incorrect

For more information on Azure Data Lake Analytics, please visit the below URL

https://docs.microsoft.com/en-us/azure/data-lake-analytics/data-lake-analytics-overview

148.   A company has setup a Virtual Machine as part of their purchase subscription. They now want to move the Virtual Machine to another subscription. Is this possible?

A. Yes

B. No

Answer – A

Explanation:

Yes, you can move Azure resources between subscriptions. Below is an example of moving a Virtual Machine across subscriptions

Move a Windows VM to another Azure subscription or resource group

09/12/2018 · 2 minutes to read · Contributors 🌑🌑🌑🌑

This article walks you through how to move a Windows virtual machine (VM) between resource groups or subscriptions. Moving between subscriptions can be handy if you originally created a VM in a personal subscription and now want to move it to your company's subscription to continue your work.

For more information on moving Azure resources, please visit the below URL

https://docs.microsoft.com/en-us/azure/azure-resource-manager/resource-group-move-resources

149.   A company has 100 machines in their on-premise environment. They want to extend their infrastructure without too much extra capital or operational expenditure. Which of the following could they opt to carry out for this requirement?

A. Migrate all to the public cloud
B. Move all to the private cloud
C. Have a hybrid architecture
D. Move just 50 machines to the public cloud

Answer – C

Explanation:

When you are looking to extend your architecture to the cloud, then the best is to have a hybrid architecture. There are different scenarios that can be adopted depending on the type of integration required. An example from the Microsoft documentation is shown below

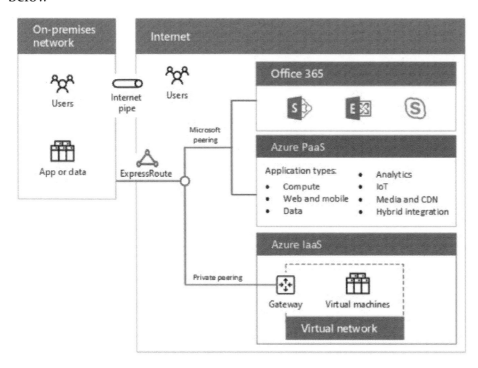

For more information on hybrid cloud overview, please visit the below URLs

https://docs.microsoft.com/en-us/office365/enterprise/hybrid-cloud-overview

https://azure.microsoft.com/en-in/overview/what-is-hybrid-cloud-computing/

A hybrid cloud is a computing environment that combines a public cloud and a private cloud by allowing data and applications to be shared between them. When computing and processing demand fluctuates, hybrid cloud computing gives businesses the ability to seamlessly scale their on-premises infrastructure up to the public cloud to handle any overflow —without giving third-party datacenters access to the entirety of their data. Organizations gain the flexibility and computing power of the public cloud for basic and non-sensitive computing tasks, while keeping business-critical applications and data on-premises, safely behind a company firewall.

Using a hybrid cloud not only allows companies to scale computing resources, it also eliminates the need to make massive capital expenditures to handle short-term spikes in demand as well as when the business needs to free up local resources for more sensitive data or applications. Companies will pay only for resources they temporarily use instead of having to purchase, program, and maintain additional resources and equipment that could remain idle over long periods of time. Hybrid cloud computing is a "best of all possible worlds" platform, delivering all the benefits of cloud computing—flexibility, scalability, and cost efficiencies—with the lowest possible risk of data exposure. Read more about hybrid cloud capabilities and getting started with Azure.

150. A company has a Virtual Machine created in their subscription. An application is installed on the Virtual Machine. You need to ensure that traffic can flow into the Virtual Machine on port 8080. Which of the following must you modify to make this work?

A. Network Interface Card

B. Network Security Group

C. Route Tables

D. Route Filters

Answer – B

Explanation:

You have to modify the Network Security Group. You have to add an Inbound Security Rule. An example is shown below

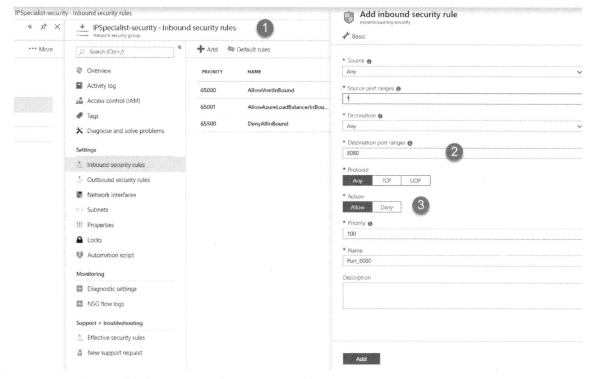

1. So first add the Inbound Security rule
2. Add the destination port range as 8080
3. Ensure the Action is Allow

Since the right implementation is via Network Security Groups, all other options are incorrect

For more information on network security groups, please visit the below URL

https://docs.microsoft.com/en-us/azure/virtual-network/security-overview

151. A company wants to migrate some scripts to Azure. They want to make use of the serverless features available in Azure

They decide to use the Azure Virtual Machine service

Would this service meet the requirement?

   A. Yes

   B. No

Answer - B

Explanation:

This is an Infrastructure as a service product and is not a serverless product. Below is what the Microsoft documentation states about this service.

Overview of Windows virtual machines in Azure

10/04/2018 • 7 minutes to read • Contributors 🟢🟢🟢🟢 all

Azure Virtual Machines (VM) is one of several types of on-demand, scalable computing resources that Azure offers. Typically, you choose a VM when you need more control over the computing environment than the other choices offer. This article gives you information about what you should consider before you create a VM, how you create it, and how you manage it.

For more information on Azure Windows Virtual Machines, please visit the below URL

https://docs.microsoft.com/en-us/azure/virtual-machines/windows/overview

152.   A company wants to migrate some scripts to Azure. They want to make use of the serverless features available in Azure

They decide to use the Azure Functions service

Would this service meet the requirement?

A. Yes

B. No

Answer – A

Explanation:

This is the right product to use. Below is what the Microsoft documentation states about this service.

An introduction to Azure Functions

10/03/2017 • 4 minutes to read • Contributors 🟢🟢🟢🟢 all

Azure Functions is a solution for easily running small pieces of code, or "functions," in the cloud. You can write just the code you need for the problem at hand, without worrying about a whole application or the infrastructure to run it. Functions can make development even more productive, and you can use your development language of choice, such as C#, F#, Node.js, Java, or PHP. Pay only for the time your code runs and trust Azure to scale as needed. Azure Functions lets you develop serverless applications on Microsoft Azure.

For more information on Azure Functions, please visit the below URL

https://docs.microsoft.com/en-us/azure/azure-functions/functions-overview

153.   A company wants to migrate some scripts to Azure. They want to make use of the serverless features available in Azure

They decide to use the Azure Content Delivery Network service

Would this service meet the requirement?

A. Yes

B. No

Answer – B

Explanation:

This service is used for delivering web content to end users. Below is what the Microsoft documentation states about this service.

What is a content delivery network on Azure?

05/09/2018 · 3 minutes to read · Contributors 🔵⚪⚫🔵🏆 all

A content delivery network (CDN) is a distributed network of servers that can efficiently deliver web content to users. CDNs store cached content on edge servers in point-of-presence (POP) locations that are close to end users, to minimize latency.

Azure Content Delivery Network (CDN) offers developers a global solution for rapidly delivering high-bandwidth content to users by caching their content at strategically placed physical nodes across the world. Azure CDN can also accelerate dynamic content, which cannot be cached, by leveraging various network optimizations using CDN POPs. For example, route optimization to bypass Border Gateway Protocol (BGP).

For more information on Azure Content Delivery Network service, please visit the below URL

https://docs.microsoft.com/en-us/azure/cdn/cdn-overview

154.   A company is planning on using an entire suite of Microsoft products. Which of the following belongs to the category of Software as a service (SaaS)?

A. Azure Virtual Machine service
B. Microsoft Office 365
C. Azure App Service
D. Azure Content Delivery Network Service

Answer – B

Explanation:

The Microsoft documentation mentions below the definition of Software as a service (SaaS)

Software as a service (SaaS) allows users to connect to and use cloud-based apps over the Internet. Common examples are email, calendaring, and office tools (such as Microsoft Office 365).

SaaS provides a complete software solution that you purchase on a pay-as-you-go basis from a cloud service provider. You rent the use of an app for your organization, and your users connect to it over the Internet, usually with a web browser. All of the underlying infrastructure, middleware, app software, and app data are located in the service provider's data center. The service provider manages the hardware and software, and with the appropriate service agreement, will ensure the availability and the security of the app and your data as well. SaaS allows your organization to get quickly up and running with an app at minimal upfront cost.

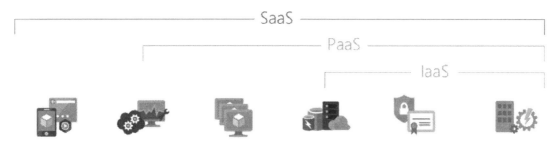

Option A is incorrect since this belongs to the category of Infrastructure as a service (IaaS)

Options C and D are incorrect since this belongs to the category of Platform as a service (PaaS)

For more information on Software as a service, please visit the below URL

https://azure.microsoft.com/en-us/overview/what-is-saas/

155.   A company has created an Azure Virtual machine as shown below

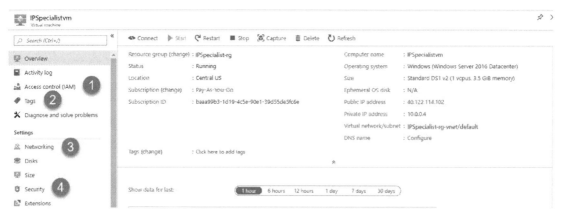

They want to ensure that a specific set of users have access to 'Stop' the virtual machine. Which of the following of the virtual machine would you use to fulfil this requirement?

   A. Access Control (IAM)

   B. Tags

   C. Networking

D. Security

Answer – A

Explanation:

If you go to the Access Control section, you can define a role assignment for a user that could conduct specific operations on the virtual machine.

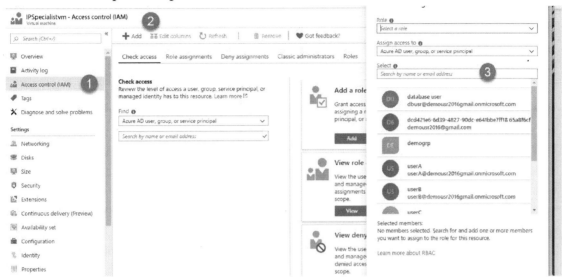

Since this is clear from the implementation, all other options are incorrect

For more information on managing access using Role Based access control, please visit the following URL

- https://docs.microsoft.com/en-us/azure/role-based-access-control/role-assignments-portal

156.   A company wants to provision a solution with the following requirements
- Provision a WordPress solution
- Host the solution on a Virtual Machine

Which of the following could be used to quickly deploy the required solution?

A. Virtual Machine Scale sets

B. Azure Resource Groups

C. Azure Marketplace

D. Azure Web Apps

Answer – C

Explanation:

You can easily search for custom solutions in the Azure Marketplace. You can so easily even deploy these solutions onto Azure.

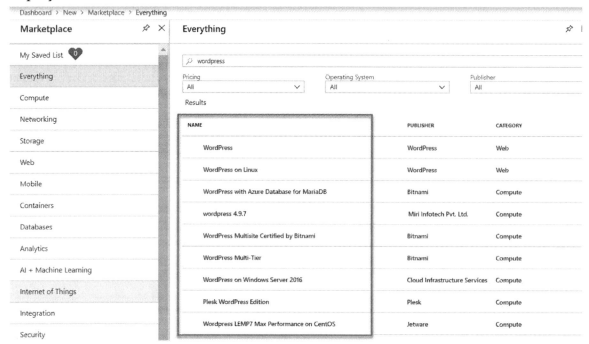

Option A is incorrect since there is no mention of the need of a scalable solution

Option B is incorrect since this used to categorize resources

Option D is incorrect since this used as a Platform as a service solution for web applications

You can visit the Azure Marketplace via the following URL

https://azuremarketplace.microsoft.com/en-us/marketplace/

157.   A company wants to host a set of tables in Azure. They want absolutely zero administration of the underlying infrastructure and low latency access to data.

You recommend using the Azure SQL Database service?

Would this suit the requirement?

   A. Yes
   B. No

Answer – A

Explanation:

Even though this is a platform as a service, Microsoft handles all patching and updating of the SQL and operating system code.

For more information on the Azure SQL Database service, please visit the below URL

https://docs.microsoft.com/en-us/azure/sql-database/sql-database-technical-overview

158.　　A company wants to host a set of Table API for applications that are written for Azure Table storage.

You recommend using the CosmosDB service?

Would this suit the requirement?

A. Yes

B. No

Answer – A

Explanation:

This service is a fully managed service and also provides low latency access to data. It also has a table API to work with Table like data

Introduction to Azure Cosmos DB: Table API

11/20/2017 · 2 minutes to read · Contributors ● ● ● ● ℛ all

Azure Cosmos DB provides the Table API for applications that are written for Azure Table storage and that need premium capabilities like:

- Turnkey global distribution.
- Dedicated throughput worldwide.
- Single-digit millisecond latencies at the 99th percentile.
- Guaranteed high availability.
- Automatic secondary indexing.

Applications written for Azure Table storage can migrate to Azure Cosmos DB by using the Table API with no code changes and take advantage of premium capabilities. The Table API has client SDKs available for .NET, Java, Python, and Node.js.

For more information on the Azure CosmosDB service – Table API, please visit the below URL

https://docs.microsoft.com/en-us/azure/cosmos-db/table-introduction

159.　　A company wants to host a set of tables in Azure. They want absolutely zero administration of the underlying infrastructure and low latency access to data.

You recommend using the Azure App service?

Would this suit the requirement?

A. Yes

B. No

Answer – B

Explanation:

This is a fully managed service for hosting web applications.

For more information on Azure Web Apps, please visit the below URL

https://docs.microsoft.com/en-us/azure/app-service/overview

160. A company wants to implement an IoT solution using the service available in Azure. Which of the following would meet the below requirement?

"Monitor and control millions of Internet of Things assets"

A. IoT Hub
B. IoT solution accelerators
C. IoT Edge
D. Azure Time Series Insights

Answer – A

Explanation:

The Microsoft documentation mentions the following

What is Azure IoT Hub?

07/04/2018 • 3 minutes to read • Contributors ● ● ●

IoT Hub is a managed service, hosted in the cloud, that acts as a central message hub for bi-directional communication between your IoT application and the devices it manages. You can use Azure IoT Hub to build IoT solutions with reliable and secure communications between millions of IoT devices and a cloud-hosted solution backend. You can connect virtually any device to IoT Hub.

Since this is clearly mentioned in the documentation, all other options are incorrect

For more information on Azure IoT Hub, please visit the below URL

https://docs.microsoft.com/en-us/azure/iot-hub/about-iot-hub

161. A company wants to implement an IoT solution using the service available in Azure. Which of the following would meet the below requirement?

"Used to analyze data on End user devices"

A. IoT Hub
B. IoT Central

C. IoT Edge

D. Azure Time Series Insights

Answer – C

Explanation:

The Microsoft documentation mentions the following

Azure IoT Edge

Azure IoT Edge is an Internet of Things (IoT) service that builds on top of IoT Hub. This service is meant for customers who want to analyze data on devices, a.k.a. "at the edge", instead of in the cloud. By moving parts of your workload to the edge, your devices can spend less time sending messages to the cloud and react more quickly to changes in status.

Since this is clearly mentioned in the documentation, all other options are incorrect

For more information on Azure IoT Edge, please visit the below URL

https://docs.microsoft.com/en-us/azure/iot-edge/

162.   A company wants to implement an IoT solution using the service available in Azure. Which of the following would meet the below requirement?

"Provide bi-directional communication between IoT application and the devices"

A. IoT Hub

B. IoT Central

C. IoT Edge

D. Azure Time Series Insights

Answer – A

Explanation:

The Microsoft documentation mentions the following

IoT Hub: This service allows you to connect from your devices to an IoT hub, and monitor and control billions of IoT devices. This is especially useful if you need bi-directional communication between your IoT devices and your back end. This is the underlying service for IoT Central and IoT solution accelerators.

What is Azure IoT Hub?

08/08/2019 • 3 minutes to read • 🌑 🌑 🌑 🌑 🌑

IoT Hub is a managed service, hosted in the cloud, that acts as a central message hub for bi-directional communication between your IoT application and the devices it manages. You can use Azure IoT Hub to build IoT solutions with reliable and secure communications between millions of IoT devices and a cloud-hosted solution backend. You can connect virtually any device to IoT Hub.

IoT Hub supports communications both from the device to the cloud and from the cloud to the device. IoT Hub supports multiple messaging patterns such as device-to-cloud telemetry, file upload from devices, and request-reply methods to control your devices from the cloud. IoT Hub monitoring helps you maintain the health of your solution by tracking events such as device creation, device failures, and device connections.

IoT Hub's capabilities help you build scalable, full-featured IoT solutions such as managing industrial equipment used in manufacturing, tracking valuable assets in healthcare, and monitoring office building usage.

Since this is clearly mentioned in the documentation, all other options are incorrect
For more information on Azure IoT , please visit the below URL
https://docs.microsoft.com/en-us/azure/iot-fundamentals/iot-introduction
https://docs.microsoft.com/en-us/azure/iot-hub/about-iot-hub

163.   A company wants to implement an IoT solution using the service available in Azure. Which of the following would meet the below requirement?

"Helps provide a powerful data exploration and telemetry tools to help you refine operational analysis"

   A. IoT Hub
   B. IoT Central
   C. IoT Edge
   D. Azure Time Series Insights

Answer – D

Explanation:

The Microsoft documentation mentions the following

Azure Time Series Insights Preview overview

12/05/2018 · 4 minutes to read · Contributors 🔵🔵🔵

Azure Time Series Insights Preview is an end-to-end platform-as-a-service offering. It's used to ingest, process, store, and query highly contextualized, time-series-optimized IoT-scale data. Time Series Insights is ideal for ad-hoc data exploration and operational analysis. Time Series Insights is a uniquely extensible and customized service offering that meets the broad needs of industrial IoT deployments.

Since this is clearly mentioned in the documentation, all other options are incorrect

For more information on Azure Time Series Insights, please visit the below URL

https://docs.microsoft.com/en-us/azure/time-series-insights/

164.   A company is planning on hosting a set of resources in Azure. They want to protect their resources against DDoS attacks and also get real time attack metrics. Which of the following should the company opt for?

A. DDoS Protection Basic

B. DDoS Protection Standard

C. DDoS Protection Premium

D. DDoS Protection Isolated

Answer - B

Explanation:

The Microsoft documentation mentions the following

Feature	DDoS Protection Basic	DDoS Protection Standard
Active traffic monitoring & always on detection	Yes	Yes
Automatic attack mitigations	Yes	Yes
Availability guarantee	Azure region	Application
Mitigation policies	Tuned for Azure region traffic volume	Tuned for application traffic volume
Metrics & alerts	No	Real time attack metrics & diagnostic logs via Azure monitor
Mitigation reports	No	Post attack mitigation reports
Mitigation flow logs	No	NRT log stream for SIEM integration
Mitigation policy customizations	No	Engage DDoS experts
Support	Best effort	Access to DDoS Experts during an active attack
SLA	Azure region	Application SLA guarantee & cost protection
Pricing	Free	Monthly & usage based

Since this is clearly mentioned in the documentation, all other options are incorrect

For more information on DDoS protection, please visit the below URL

https://docs.microsoft.com/en-us/azure/virtual-network/ddos-protection-overview

165.   You are planning on setting up an Azure Free Account. By setting up an Azure Free Account, would you only get access to a subset of services?

A. Yes

B. No

Answer – B

Explanation:

The Azure Free Account gives access to all services in Azure. This is also mentioned in the FAQ section for the Azure Free Account

Can the Azure free account be used for production or only for development?

The Azure free account provides access to all Azure products and does not block customers from building their ideas into production. The Azure free account includes certain products—and specific quantities of those products—for free. To enable your production scenarios, you may need to use resources beyond the free amounts. You'll be billed for those additional resources at the pay-as-you-go rates.

For more information on the common asked questions for the Azure Free account, please visit the below URL

https://azure.microsoft.com/en-us/free/free-account-faq/

166.   You are planning on setting up an Azure Free Account. Would the credit in the Azure Free Account expire after a specific period of time?

A. Yes

B. No

Answer – A

Explanation:

After a duration of 30 days or if the 200 USD credit gets over, then you have to convert your Free subscription to a Pay-As-You-Go subscription.

This is also mentioned in the FAQ section for the Azure Free Account

What does it mean to upgrade my account?

When you sign up for an Azure free account, you get a $200 credit that acts as a spending limit—that is, in the first 30 days, any usage of resources beyond the free products and quantities will be deducted from the $200 credit. When you've used up the $200 credit or 30 days have expired (whichever happens first), you'll have to upgrade to a pay-as-you-go account. This automatically removes the spending limit so you can continue to get access to all the free products included in the free account. With the spending limit removed, you pay for what you use beyond the free amounts and this is charged to the card you provided.

For more information on the common asked questions for the Azure Free account, please visit the below URL

167.   Your company has just setup an Azure subscription and Azure tenant with VMs in place. They want to have recommendations given by the Azure Advisor tool. Is it possible for the Azure Advisor tool to give a list of Azure virtual machines that are currently not enabled by Azure Backup?

A. Yes

B. No

Answer - A

Explanation:

Advisor identifies virtual machines where backup is not enabled, and it recommends enabling backup.

For more information on the high availability requirements provides by the Azure Advisor tool, please visit the below URL

https://docs.microsoft.com/en-us/azure/advisor/advisor-high-availability-recommendations

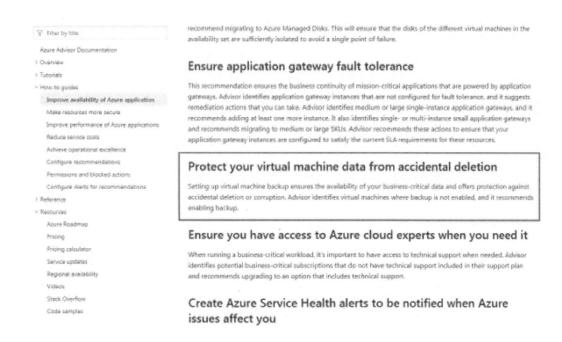

168.   Your company has just set up an Azure subscription and an Azure tenant. They want to use recommendations given by the Azure Advisor tool. If your

company starts implementing the recommendations given by the Azure Advisor tool, would the company's security score decrease?

A. Yes

B. No

Answer – B

Explanation:

If you improve the security stance of your resources, your security score will increase.

The security score is maintained in Azure Security Center.

For more information on the Azure Security Center score, please visit the below URL

https://docs.microsoft.com/en-us/azure/security-center/security-center-secure-score

169. Your company has just setup an Azure subscription and an Azure tenant. Is it mandatory for the company to implement all Azure security recommendations within a period of 30 days in order to maintain Microsoft support?

A. Yes

B. No

Answer – B

Explanation:

Microsoft provides the required controls for the customer to implement secure practices for their Azure account. There is no constraint which mentions that you need to implement all security recommendations to maintain Microsoft support

The Microsoft documentation gives a briefing on the Shared responsibility model that needs to be understood by the customer.

Shared responsibility model

It's important to understand the division of responsibility between you and Microsoft. On-premises, you own the whole stack, but as you move to the cloud, some responsibilities transfer to Microsoft. The following graphic illustrates the areas of responsibility, according to the type of deployment of your stack (software as a service [SaaS], platform as a service [PaaS], infrastructure as a service [IaaS], and on-premises).

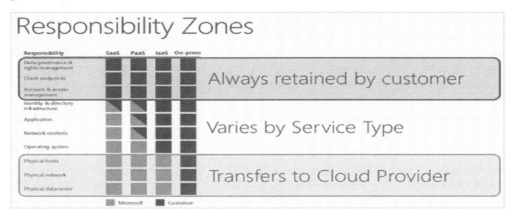

For more information on the fundamentals on Azure Infrastructure security, please visit the below URL

https://docs.microsoft.com/en-us/azure/security/fundamentals/infrastructure

170.   Your company is planning on setting up an Azure subscription and an Azure tenant using Azure Active Directory. Would the company need to implement domain controllers on Azure virtual machines to use the Azure AD service?

A. Yes

B. No

Answer - B

Explanation:

Azure Active Directory is a completely managed service. You don't need to provision any infrastructure to implement Azure Active Directory

For more information on Azure Active Directory, please visit the below URL

https://docs.microsoft.com/en-us/azure/active-directory/fundamentals/active-directory-whatis

171. Your company is planning on setting up an Azure subscription and an Azure tenant using Azure Active Directory. Does Azure Active Directory provide authentication services for services hosted in Azure and Microsoft Office 365?

A. Yes

B. No

Answer - A

Explanation:

You can use Azure Active Directory to authenticate to both Azure based resources and also to Microsoft office 365

The Microsoft documentation mentions the following

What is Azure Active Directory?

07/31/2019 • 9 minutes to read • 🌐 🔵 ⚫ 🔲 🔲 +8

Azure Active Directory (Azure AD) is Microsoft's cloud-based identity and access management service, which helps your employees sign in and access resources in:

- External resources, such as Microsoft Office 365, the Azure portal, and thousands of other SaaS applications.

- Internal resources, such as apps on your corporate network and intranet, along with any cloud apps developed by your own organization.

You can use the various Microsoft Cloud for Enterprise Architects Series posters to better understand the core identity services in Azure, Azure AD, and Office 365.

For more information on Azure Active Directory, please visit the below URL

https://docs.microsoft.com/en-us/azure/active-directory/fundamentals/active-directory-whatis

172. A company is planning on setting up an Azure subscription and an Azure tenant using Azure Active Directory. When assigning product licences to Azure Active Directory users, would a user be limited to the assignment of a single product licence only?

A. Yes

B. No

Answer – B

Explanation:

You can assign multiple licences for a user in Azure Active Directory.

As shown below for each user, you can assign a license depending on what licences have been purchased

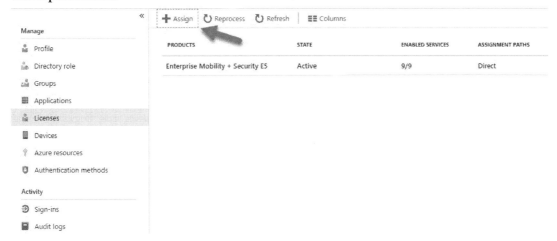

For more information on adding licences in Azure Active Directory, please visit the below URL

https://docs.microsoft.com/en-us/azure/active-directory/fundamentals/license-users-groups

173.   A team has an object named audio.log stored in the Blob service in the Azure storage account. A partial snapshot of the properties is given below

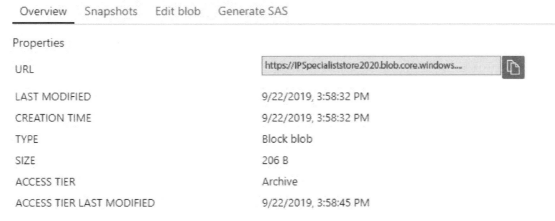

Which of the following needs to be done before the object can be accessed?

 A. Create a snapshot of the object

 B. Rehydrate the object

 C. Change the type of the object

D. Change the URL of the object

Answer – B

Explanation:

The Blob object is in the Archive tier as shown below

Overview   Snapshots   Edit blob   Generate SAS

Properties

URL	https://IPSpecialiststore2020.blob.core.windows....
LAST MODIFIED	9/22/2019, 3:58:32 PM
CREATION TIME	9/22/2019, 3:58:32 PM
TYPE	Block blob
SIZE	206 B
ACCESS TIER	Archive
ACCESS TIER LAST MODIFIED	9/22/2019, 3:58:45 PM

In order to access the object, you first need to hydrate the object.
The Microsoft documentation mentions the following

Blob rehydration

To read data in archive storage, you must first change the tier of the blob to hot or cool. This process is known as rehydration and can take hours to complete. We recommend large blob sizes for optimal rehydration performance. Rehydrating several small blobs concurrently may add additional time. There are currently two rehydrate priorities, High (preview) and Standard, which can be set via the optional *x-ms-rehydrate-priority* property on a <u>Set Blob Tier</u> or <u>Copy Blob</u> operation.

Since this is clear from the documentation, all other options are incorrect
For more information on Storage blob access tiers, please visit the below URL
https://docs.microsoft.com/en-us/azure/storage/blobs/storage-blob-storage-tiers

174.   A company is planning on storing 1 TB of data in Azure BLOB storage. Would the cost of data storage be the same regardless of the region the data is stored in?

A. Yes
B. No

Answer – B

Explanation:

When you look at the pricing for Azure BLOB storage, there is a selector for the region. The cost depends on the region the BLOB is located in.

Redundancy:	Region:	Currency:
LRS ▾	Central US ▾	US Dollar ($) ▾

Pricing offers: Recommended   Blob only   Other

Data storage prices

All prices are per GB, per month.

	PREMIUM	HOT	COOL	ARCHIVE˙
First 50 terabyte (TB) / month	$0.18 per GB	$0.0184 per GB	$0.01 per GB	$0.002 per GB
Next 450 TB / Month	$0.18 per GB	$0.0177 per GB	$0.01 per GB	$0.002 per GB
Over 500 TB / Month	$0.18 per GB	$0.0170 per GB	$0.01 per GB	$0.002 per GB

For more information on Azure BLOB pricing, please visit the below URL

https://azure.microsoft.com/en-us/pricing/details/storage/blobs/

175.   A company is planning on using an Azure storage account. They are planning on provisioning an Azure storage account of the kind "General Purpose v2". Would the company be charged only for the amount of data stored and not for the amount of read and write operations?

A. Yes
B. No

Answer – B

Explanation:

The cost of Azure storage depends on several factors, and one of them includes the number of read and write operations.

The Microsoft documentation mentions the following when it comes to an example of pricing for Block Blob storage.

Block blob storage is used for streaming and storing documents, videos, pictures, backups, and other unstructured text or binary data.

Total cost of block blob storage depends on:

- Volume of data stored per month.
- Quantity and types of operations performed, along with any data transfer costs.
- Data redundancy option selected.

For more information on Azure BLOB pricing, please visit the below URL

https://azure.microsoft.com/en-us/pricing/details/storage/blobs/

176.   A company is planning on setting up a string of Azure Storage Accounts. Is the transfer of data between Azure storage accounts in different Azure regions free of cost?

A. Yes
B. No

Answer – B

Explanation:

All services that do cross regional data transfers are subjected to a cost.

A snippet of the cost from the Microsoft documentation is given below

Pricing details

Inbound data transfers

(i.e. data going into Azure data centers): **Free**

Outbound data transfers

(i.e. data going out of Azure data centers; zones refer to source region):

OUTBOUND DATA TRANSFERS	ZONE 1*
First 5 GB /Month [1]	Free
5 GB - 10 TB [2] /Month	$0.087 per GB
Next 40 TB (10 - 50 TB) /Month	$0.083 per GB
Next 100 TB (50 - 150 TB) /Month	$0.07 per GB

For more information on Azure bandwidth pricing details, please visit the below URL https://azure.microsoft.com/en-us/pricing/details/bandwidth/

177.   A company wants to start using Azure services. They have several departments that would need to make use of Azure services. They want to give the ability for each department to use a different payment option for the amount of Azure services they consume. Which of the following should each department use to fulfil this requirement?

A. A resource group

B. A subscription

C. An Azure policy

D. A reservation

Answer – B

Explanation:

The billing for Azure resources is tagged to a subscription. Hence to segregate the billing for each department, each of them can have a different subscription.

For more information on subscriptions, please visit the below URL which refers to a blog article on the benefits of a Windows subscription

https://blogs.msdn.microsoft.com/arunrakwal/2012/04/09/create-windows-azure-subscription/

178.   A company has just setup an Azure subscription and an Azure tenant. Which of the following can the company use to create an Azure support request?

The Knowledge Center

The Azure Portal

Support.microsoft.com

The Security and Compliance admin center

Answer – B

Explanation:

You can create a support request in the Azure portal itself as shown below

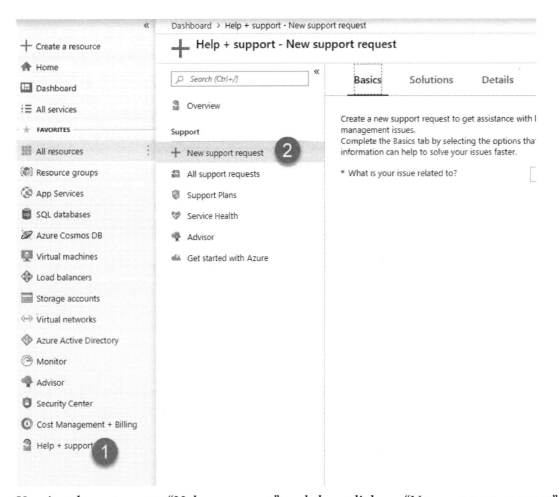

You just have to go to "Help + support" and then click on "New support request"

Since this is clear from the implementation, all other options are incorrect

For more information on creating a support request, please visit the below URL

https://docs.microsoft.com/en-us/azure/azure-supportability/how-to-create-azure-support-request

179.   Your company wants to provision a set of Azure virtual machines. An application will be installed on these virtual machines. The company wants to ensure that the user traffic is distributed across the virtual machines.

You decide to use the Azure VPN Gateway service for traffic distribution.

Would this fulfil the requirement?

   A. Yes

   B. No

Answer – B

Explanation:

This service is used to help connect an on-premise data center to an Azure virtual Network

The Microsoft documentation mentions the following

What is VPN Gateway?

05/22/2019 • 13 minutes to read • 🔵 🔵 🞉 🔵 🔵 +3

A VPN gateway is a specific type of virtual network gateway that is used to send encrypted traffic between an Azure virtual network and an on-premises location over the public Internet. You can also use a VPN gateway to send encrypted traffic between Azure virtual networks over the Microsoft network. Each virtual network can have only one VPN gateway. However, you can create multiple connections to the same VPN gateway. When you create multiple connections to the same VPN gateway, all VPN tunnels share the available gateway bandwidth.

For more information on the Azure VPN gateway, please visit the below URL

https://docs.microsoft.com/en-us/azure/vpn-gateway/vpn-gateway-about-vpngateways

180.   Your company wants to provision a set of Azure virtual machines. An application will be installed on these virtual machines. The company wants to ensure that the user traffic is distributed across the virtual machines.

You decide to use the Azure Load Balancer service for traffic distribution.

Would this fulfil the requirement?

A. Yes

B. No

Answer – A

Explanation:

The Azure Load Balancer is the ideal service to use for this scenario. It can be used to distribute traffic to the backend virtual machines.

The Microsoft documentation mentions the following

Why use Load Balancer? ⬦

You can use Azure Load Balancer to:

- Load-balance incoming internet traffic to your VMs. This configuration is known as a Public Load Balancer.
- Load-balance traffic across VMs inside a virtual network. You can also reach a Load Balancer front end from an on-premises network in a hybrid scenario. Both scenarios use a configuration that is known as an Internal Load Balancer.
- Port forward traffic to a specific port on specific VMs with inbound network address translation (NAT) rules.
- Provide outbound connectivity for VMs inside your virtual network by using a public Load Balancer.

For more information on the Azure Load Balancer, please visit the below URL

https://docs.microsoft.com/en-us/azure/load-balancer/load-balancer-overview

181. Your company wants to provision a set of Azure virtual machines. An application will be installed on these virtual machines. The company wants to ensure that the user traffic is distributed across the virtual machines.

You decide to use the Azure HDInsight service for traffic distribution.

Would this fulfil the requirement?

A. Yes

B. No

Answer – B

Explanation:

The Azure HDInsight service is used for implementing Big Data related open source frameworks.

The Microsoft documentation mentions the following

What is Azure HDInsight?

06/11/2019 • 6 minutes to read • 🔵🔵🔵

Azure HDInsight is a managed, full-spectrum, open-source analytics service in the cloud for enterprises. You can use open-source frameworks such as Hadoop, Apache Spark, Apache Hive, LLAP, Apache Kafka, Apache Storm, R, and more.

For more information on the Azure HDInsight, please visit the below URL

182.   A company is planning on setting up a solution on the Azure platform. The solution has the following main key requirement

- Provide a managed toolset that could be used to manage and scale container-based applications

Which of the following would be best suited for this requirement?

    A. Azure Event Grid

    B. Azure DevOps

    C. Azure Kubernetes

    D. Azure DevTest Labs

Answer – C

Explanation:

This can be achieved with the Azure Kubernetes service.

The Microsoft documentation mentions the following

Ship faster, operate with ease, and scale confidently

The fully managed Azure Kubernetes Service (AKS) makes deploying and managing containerized applications easy. It offers serverless Kubernetes, an integrated continuous integration and continuous delivery (CI/CD) experience, and enterprise-grade security and governance. Unite your development and operations teams on a single platform to rapidly build, deliver, and scale applications with confidence.

Since this is clearly mentioned in the documentation, all other options are incorrect

For more information on the Azure Kubernetes service, please visit the below URL

https://azure.microsoft.com/en-us/services/kubernetes-service/

183.   A company is planning on setting up a solution on the Azure platform. The solution has the following main key requirement

- Provide a continuous Integration and Delivery toolset that could work with a variety of languages

Which of the following would be best suited for this requirement?

    A. Azure Event Grid

    B. Azure DevOps

    C. Azure Kubernetes

D. Azure DevTest Labs

Answer – B

Explanation:

This can be achieved with the Azure DevOps service.

The Microsoft documentation mentions the following

Use all the DevOps services or choose just what you need to complement your existing workflows

Azure Boards

Deliver value to your users faster using proven agile tools to plan, track, and discuss work across your teams.

Learn more >

Azure Pipelines

Build, test, and deploy with CI/CD that works with any language, platform, and cloud. Connect to GitHub or any other Git provider and deploy continuously.

Learn more >

Azure Repos

Get unlimited, cloud-hosted private Git repos and collaborate to build better code with pull requests and advanced file management.

Learn more >

Since this is clearly mentioned in the documentation, all other options are incorrect

For more information on the Azure DevOps service, please visit the below URL

https://azure.microsoft.com/en-us/services/devops/

184.   A company is planning on setting up a solution on the Azure platform. The solution has the following main key requirement

- Provide a service that could be used to quickly provision development and test environments
- Minimize waste on resources with the help of quotas and policies

Which of the following would be best suited for this requirement?

A. Azure Event Grid

B. Azure DevOps

C. Azure Kubernetes

D. Azure DevTest Labs

Answer – D

Explanation:

This can be achieved with the Azure DevTest Labs service.

The Microsoft documentation mentions the following

Since this is clearly mentioned in the documentation, all other options are incorrect

For more information on the Azure DevTest Labs service, please visit the below URL

https://azure.microsoft.com/en-us/services/devtest-lab/

185.   A company is planning on setting up a solution on the Azure platform. The solution has the following main key requirement

• Be able to collect events from multiple sources and then relay them to an application

Which of the following would be best suited for this requirement?

A. Azure Event Grid

B. Azure DevOps

C. Azure Kubernetes

D. Azure DevTest Labs

Answer – A

Explanation:

This can be achieved with the Azure Event Grid service.

The Microsoft documentation mentions the following

Use Event Grid to power your event-driven and serverless apps

Simplify your event-based apps with Event Grid, a single service for managing routing of all events from any source to any destination. Designed for high availability, consistent performance, and dynamic scale, Event Grid lets you focus on your app logic rather than infrastructure.

Since this is clearly mentioned in the documentation, all other options are incorrect

For more information on the Azure Event Grid service, please visit the below URL

https://azure.microsoft.com/en-us/services/event-grid/

186.   A company is planning on using the Azure Firewall service. Would the Azure firewall service encrypt all network traffic sent from Azure to the Internet?
A. Yes
B. No

Answer – B

Explanation:

The Azure Firewall service is primarily used to protect your network infrastructure.

The Microsoft documentation mentions the following

What is Azure Firewall?

09/04/2019 • 8 minutes to read •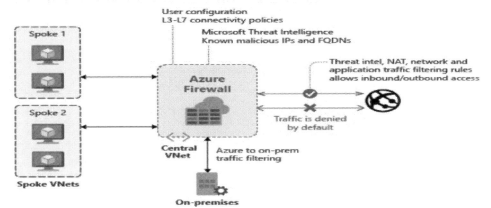

Azure Firewall is a managed, cloud-based network security service that protects your Azure Virtual Network resources. It's a fully stateful firewall as a service with built-in high availability and unrestricted cloud scalability.

You can centrally create, enforce, and log application and network connectivity policies across subscriptions and virtual networks. Azure Firewall uses a static public IP address for your virtual network resources allowing outside firewalls to identify traffic originating from your virtual network. The service is fully integrated with Azure Monitor for logging and analytics.

For more information on the Azure Firewall service, please visit the below URL

https://docs.microsoft.com/en-us/azure/firewall/overview

187.   A company is planning on using Network Security Groups. Could network security groups be used to encrypt all network traffic sent from Azure to the Internet?

A. Yes

B. No

Answer – B

Explanation:

Network Security Groups are used to restrict Inbound and Outbound traffic. It can't be used to encrypt traffic.

The Microsoft documentation mentions the following

Security groups

07/26/2018 · 25 minutes to read · ●●●● ✦ +11

You can filter network traffic to and from Azure resources in an Azure virtual network with a network security group. A network security group contains security rules that allow or deny inbound network traffic to, or outbound network traffic from, several types of Azure resources. To learn about which Azure resources can be deployed into a virtual network and have network security groups associated to them, see Virtual network integration for Azure services. For each rule, you can specify source and destination, port, and protocol.

For more information on the Azure network security, please visit the below URL

https://docs.microsoft.com/en-us/azure/virtual-network/security-overview

188.　　　A company is planning on deploying an Azure Windows Server 2016 virtual machine. Could a VPN be used to encrypt all traffic from the virtual machine itself to a host on the Internet?

A. Yes

B. No

Answer – A

Explanation:

You can install roles such as the Remote Access Server for VPN to ensure traffic is encrypted when it flows out of the server.

An example in the Microsoft documentation is given via the below URL

https://docs.microsoft.com/en-us/windows-server/remote/remote-access/vpn/always-on-vpn/deploy/vpn-deploy-ras

189.　　　You are planning on deploying an Azure virtual machine. Which of the following storage service is used to store the data disks for the virtual machine?

A. Blob

B. Files

C. Tables

D. Queues

Answer – A

Explanation:

The data disks are stored in the Blob service of Azure storage accounts.

The Microsoft documentation mentions the following

Blobs

Azure Storage supports three types of blobs:

- **Block blobs** store text and binary data, up to about 4.7 TB. Block blobs are made up of blocks of data that can be managed individually.
- **Append blobs** are made up of blocks like block blobs, but are optimized for append operations. Append blobs are ideal for scenarios such as logging data from virtual machines.
- **Page blobs** store random access files up to 8 TB in size. Page blobs store virtual hard drive (VHD) files and serve as disks for Azure virtual machines. For more information about page blobs, see Overview of Azure page blobs

Since this is clearly mentioned in the documentation, all other options are incorrect

For more information on the Azure Blob storage, please visit the below URL

https://docs.microsoft.com/en-us/azure/storage/blobs/storage-blobs-introduction

https://docs.microsoft.com/en-us/azure/virtual-machines/windows/managed-disks-overview

190.   A company currently has the following unused resources as part of their subscription

- 10 user accounts in Azure AD
- 5 user groups in Azure AD
- 10 public IP address
- 10 network Interfaces

They want to reduce the costs for resources hosted in Azure

They decide to remove the user accounts from Azure AD

Would this fulfil the requirement?

A. Yes
B. No

Answer – B

Explanation:

When you look at the pricing for Azure Active Directory, you can create 5,00,000 objects as part of the free version. These objects include both users and groups.

The Microsoft documentation mentions the following

	FREE	OFFICE 365 APPS	PREMIUM P1	PREMIUM P2
Core Identity and Access Management				
Directory Objects[1]	5,00,000 Object Limit	No Object Limit	No Object Limit	No Object Limit

For more information on the pricing for Azure Active Directory, please visit the below URL

https://azure.microsoft.com/en-in/pricing/details/active-directory/

191. A company currently has the following unused resources as part of their subscription

- 10 user accounts in Azure AD
- 5 user groups in Azure AD
- 10 public IP address
- 10 network Interfaces

They want to reduce the costs for resources hosted in Azure

They decide to remove the user groups from Azure AD

Would this fulfil the requirement?

A. Yes
B. No

Answer – B

Explanation:

When you look at the pricing for Azure Active Directory, you can create 5,00,000 objects as part of the free version. These objects include both users and groups.

The Microsoft documentation mentions the following

	FREE	OFFICE 365 APPS	PREMIUM P1	PREMIUM P2
Core Identity and Access Management				
Directory Objects[1]	5,00,000 Object Limit	No Object Limit	No Object Limit	No Object Limit

For more information on the pricing for Azure Active Directory, please visit the below URL

https://azure.microsoft.com/en-in/pricing/details/active-directory/

192. A company currently has the following unused resources as part of their subscription

- 10 user accounts in Azure AD
- 5 user groups in Azure AD
- 10 public IP address
- 10 network Interfaces

They want to reduce the costs for resources hosted in Azure

They decide to remove the public IP addresses

Would this fulfil the requirement?

   A. Yes
   B. No

Answer – A

Explanation:

Yes, this can reduce the cost since there is a price for Public IP addressing as given in the Microsoft documentation below

TYPE	BASIC (CLASSIC)	BASIC (ARM)	STANDARD (ARM)
Dynamic IP address	First Cloud Service VIP: Free Additional: $0.0036/hour[1]	$0.004/hour	N/A
Static IP address (reservation + usage)	First 5: Free Additional: $0.0036/hour	First 5: $0.004/hour[2] Additional: $0.008/hour	$0.005/hour
Public IP prefix[3]	N/A	N/A	$0.006 per IP/hour[4]

For more information on the pricing for IP addresses, please visit the below URL

https://azure.microsoft.com/th-th/pricing/details/ip-addresses/

193.   A company currently has the following unused resources as part of their subscription

- 10 user accounts in Azure AD
- 5 user groups in Azure AD
- 10 public IP address
- 10 network Interfaces

They want to reduce the costs for resources hosted in Azure

They decide to remove the network interfaces from Azure AD

Would this fulfil the requirement?

   A. Yes
   B. No

Answer – B

Explanation:

There is no price for network interfaces, so this would not help reduce the cost.

For more information on the pricing for the virtual network in Azure, please visit the below URL

https://azure.microsoft.com/en-us/pricing/details/virtual-network/

194. A company has just started using Azure. They have just acquired a subscription and created an Azure tenant. Where do they have to go to create users and groups for their Azure AD tenant?

A. App Services

B. Azure Active Directory

C. Advisor

D. Cost Management + Billing

Answer – B

Explanation:

You can create users and groups in Azure Active Directory

The Microsoft documentation mentions the following

What is Azure Active Directory?

07/31/2019 • 9 minutes to read • 😀 🌑 ⬤ 🌫 🐷 +8

Azure Active Directory (Azure AD) is Microsoft's cloud-based identity and access management service, which helps your employees sign in and access resources in:

- External resources, such as Microsoft Office 365, the Azure portal, and thousands of other SaaS applications.

- Internal resources, such as apps on your corporate network and intranet, along with any cloud apps developed by your own organization.

The other services can't be used to create users and groups

For more information on Azure Active Directory, please visit the below URL

https://docs.microsoft.com/en-us/azure/active-directory/fundamentals/active-directory-whatis

195.   A company is planning on moving some of their on-premise resources to Azure. They have to provide a business justification for moving to Azure. They have to classify expenses as part of the business justification. Which category would the following expenses come under?

"Software Licence renewals"

A. Primary Expenditure

B. Capital Expenditure

C. Secondary Expenditure

D. Operating Expenditure

Answer – D

Explanation:

This expense comes under the operational expense category, reason we need to purchase the licenses while working at on-premises and when we move to cloud, we have the facility of using the same licenses.

The Microsoft documentation gives examples of operating expenses

OpEx cloud computing costs

With cloud computing, many of the costs associated with an on-premises datacenter are shifted to the service provider. Instead of thinking about physical hardware and datacenter costs, cloud computing has a different set of costs. For accounting purposes, all these costs are operational expenses:

Leasing software and customized features

Using a pay-per-use model requires actively managing your subscriptions to ensure users do not misuse the services, and that provisioned accounts are being utilized and not wasted. As soon as the provider provisions resources, billing starts. It is your responsibility to de-provision the resources when they aren't in use so that you can minimize costs.

Scaling charges based on usage/demand instead of fixed hardware or capacity.

Cloud computing can bill in various ways, such as the number of users or CPU usage time. However, billing categories can also include allocated RAM, I/O operations per second (IOPS), and storage space. Plan for backup traffic and data recovery traffic to determine the bandwidth needed.

Billing at the user or organization level.

The subscription (pay-per-use) model is a computing billing method that is designed for both organizations and users. The organization or user is billed for the services used, typically on a recurring basis. You can scale, customize, and provision computing resources, including software, storage, and development platforms. For example, when using a dedicated cloud service, you could pay based on server hardware and usage.

For more information on financial models, please visit the below URL

https://docs.microsoft.com/en-us/learn/modules/principles-cloud-computing/3c-capex-vs-opex

196.   A company is planning on moving some of their on-premise resources to Azure. They have to provide a business justification for moving to Azure. They have to classify expenses as part of the business justification. Which category would the following expense come under?

"Cooling expenses"

A. Primary Expenditure

B. Capital Expenditure

C. Secondary Expenditure

D. Operating Expenditure

Answer - D

Explanation:

This expense comes under the operating expense category.

The Microsoft documentation gives examples of operating expenses

Operational cost reductions

Recurring expenses required to operate a business are often called operating expenses. This is a broad category. In most accounting models, it includes:

- Software licensing.
- Hosting expenses.
- Electric bills.
- Real estate rentals.
- Cooling expenses.
- Temporary staff required for operations.
- Equipment rentals.
- Replacement parts.
- Maintenance contracts.
- Repair services.
- Business continuity and disaster recovery (BCDR) services.
- Other expenses that don't require capital expense approvals.

Since this is clearly mentioned in the documentation, all other options are incorrect

For more information on financial models, please visit the below URL

https://docs.microsoft.com/en-us/azure/architecture/cloud-adoption/business-strategy/financial-models

197.   A company is planning on moving some of their on-premise resources to Azure. They have to provide a business justification for moving to Azure. They have to classify expenses as part of the business justification. Which category would the following expense come under?

"New On-premise performance cluster to host a Big Data solution"

A. Primary Expenditure

B. Capital Expenditure

C. Secondary Expenditure

D. Operating Expenditure

Answer – B

Explanation:

This expense comes under the capital expense category.

The Microsoft documentation gives examples of capital expenses

Capital expense reductions or avoidance

Capital expenses are slightly different from operating expenses. Generally, this category is driven by refresh cycles or datacenter expansion. An example of a datacenter expansion would be a new high-performance cluster to host a big data solution or data warehouse. This expense would generally fit into a capital expense category. More common are the basic refresh cycles. Some companies have rigid hardware refresh cycles, meaning assets are retired and replaced on a regular cycle (usually every three, five, or eight years). These cycles often coincide with asset lease cycles or the forecasted life span of equipment. When a refresh cycle hits, IT draws capital expense to acquire new equipment.

If a refresh cycle is approved and budgeted, the cloud transformation could help eliminate that cost. If a refresh cycle is planned but not yet approved, the cloud transformation could avoid a capital expenditure. Both reductions would be added to the cost delta.

Since this is clearly mentioned in the documentation, all other options are incorrect

For more information on financial models, please visit the below URL

https://docs.microsoft.com/en-us/azure/architecture/cloud-adoption/business-strategy/financial-models

198. A company has just setup an Azure subscription and an Azure tenant. They want to start deploying resources on the Azure platform. They want to implement a way to logically group the resources. Which of the following could be used for this requirement?

A. Availability Zones

B. Azure Resource Groups

C. Azure Resource Manager

D. Azure Regions

Answer – B

Explanation:

This can be done with the help of resources groups.

The Microsoft documentation mentions the following

What is an Azure resource group?

Each resource in Azure must belong to a <u>resource group</u>. A resource group is simply a logical construct that groups multiple resources together so they can be managed as a single entity. For example, resources that share a similar lifecycle, such as the resources for an <u>n-tier application</u> may be created or deleted as a group.

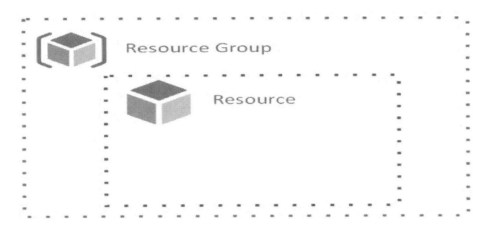

Since this is clearly mentioned in the documentation, all other options are incorrect

For more information on resources and resource group, please visit the below URL

https://docs.microsoft.com/en-us/azure/architecture/cloud-adoption/governance/resource-consistency/azure-resource-access

199. A company has just setup an Azure subscription and an Azure tenant. They want to start deploying resources on the Azure platform. They want to implement a way to deploy the resources so that they would be located closest to the users accessing those resources. Which of the following could be used for this requirement?

A. Availability Zones

B. Azure Resource Groups

C. Azure Resource Manager

D. Azure Regions

Answer – D

Explanation:

You can make use of Azure Regions and deploy the resources to the region that is closest to the user.

The Microsoft documentation mentions the following

Since this is clearly mentioned in the documentation, all other options are incorrect

For more information on Azure Regions, please visit the below URL

https://azure.microsoft.com/en-us/global-infrastructure/regions/

200. A company has just setup an Azure subscription and an Azure tenant. They want to start deploying resources on the Azure platform. They want to use an Azure service that could be used to create and update the resources as a group, rather than handling them individually, within the Azure subscription.

Which of the following could be used for this requirement?

A. Availability Zones

B. Azure Resource Groups

C. Azure Resource Manager

D. Azure Regions

Answer – C

Explanation:

This can be done with the help of the Azure Resource Manager

The Microsoft documentation mentions the following

Azure Resource Manager overview

08/29/2019 • 5 minutes to read • 🔵 🔴 🔲 🔴 🟢 +7

Azure Resource Manager is the deployment and management service for Azure. It provides a management layer that enables you to create, update, and delete resources in your Azure subscription. You use management features, like access control, locks, and tags, to secure and organize your resources after deployment.

The benefits of using Resource Manager

With Resource Manager, you can:

- Manage your infrastructure through declarative templates rather than scripts.

- Deploy, manage, and monitor all the resources for your solution as a group, rather than handling these resources individually.

- Redeploy your solution throughout the development lifecycle and have confidence your resources are deployed in a consistent state.

- Define the dependencies between resources so they're deployed in the correct order.

- Apply access control to all services in your resource group because Role-Based Access Control (RBAC) is natively integrated into the management platform.

- Apply tags to resources to logically organize all the resources in your subscription.

- Clarify your organization's billing by viewing costs for a group of resources sharing the same tag.

Since this is clearly mentioned in the documentation, all other options are incorrect

For more information on Azure Resource Manager, please visit the below URL

https://docs.microsoft.com/en-us/azure/azure-resource-manager/resource-group-overview

201.   A company is planning on setting up an database on Azure SQL database service. Would the company administrative team have full control over the underlying server hosting the Azure SQL database?

A. Yes

B. No

Answer – B

Explanation:

The Azure SQL database service is a Platform as a service. Here the underlying infrastructure is completely managed by Azure.

The Microsoft documentation mentions the following

What is the Azure SQL Database service?

04/08/2019 • 20 minutes to read • 👤 👤👤👤👤 +21

Azure SQL Database is a general-purpose relational database, provided as a managed service. With it, you can create a highly available and high-performance data storage layer for the applications and solutions in Azure. SQL Database can be the right choice for a variety of modern cloud applications because it enables you to process both relational data and non-relational structures, such as graphs, JSON, spatial, and XML.

For more information on Azure SQL database, please visit the below URL

https://docs.microsoft.com/en-us/azure/sql-database/sql-database-technical-overview

202. Would a company's administrative team have full control over a virtual machine to install an application?

A. Yes

B. No

Answer – A

Explanation:

The Azure virtual machine service is an Infrastructure as a service. Here you can install applications on the underlying virtual machine.

The Microsoft documentation mentions the following

Overview of Windows virtual machines in Azure

10/04/2018 • 7 minutes to read • 👤👤👤👤👤 +7

Azure Virtual Machines (VM) is one of several types of on-demand, scalable computing resources that Azure offers. Typically, you choose a VM when you need more control over the computing environment than the other choices offer. This article gives you information about what you should consider before you create a VM, how you create it, and how you manage it.

An Azure VM gives you the flexibility of virtualization without having to buy and maintain the physical hardware that runs it. However, you still need to maintain the VM by performing tasks, such as configuring, patching, and installing the software that runs on it.

For more information on Azure virtual machines, please visit the below URL

https://docs.microsoft.com/en-us/azure/virtual-machines/windows/overview

203.   A company is planning on deploying a web application to the Azure Web App service. Would the company administrative team have full control over the underlying machine hosting the web application?

A. Yes

B. No

Answer – B

Explanation:

The Azure Web App service is Platform as a service. Here the underlying infrastructure is completely managed by Azure.

The Microsoft documentation mentions the following

App Service overview

01/04/2017 · 2 minutes to read · ●●● ⋒ ●

Azure App Service is an HTTP-based service for hosting web applications, REST APIs, and mobile back ends. You can develop in your favorite language, be it .NET, .NET Core, Java, Ruby, Node.js, PHP, or Python. Applications run and scale with ease on both Windows and Linux-based environments. For Linux-based environments, see App Service on Linux.

App Service not only adds the power of Microsoft Azure to your application, such as security, load balancing, autoscaling, and automated management. You can also take advantage of its DevOps capabilities, such as continuous deployment from Azure DevOps, GitHub, Docker Hub, and other sources, package management, staging environments, custom domain, and SSL certificates.

For more information on Azure App Service, please visit the below URL

https://docs.microsoft.com/en-us/azure/app-service/overview

204.   You have just setup a Windows virtual machine in Azure. The machine is currently in the stopped state. The details of the machine are given below

Resource group (change) IPSpecialist-rg	Computer name (start VM to view)
Status Stopped (deallocated)	Operating system Windows
Location Central US	Size Standard DS1 v2 (1 vcpus, 3.5 GiB memory)
Subscription (change) Pay-As-You-Go	Ephemeral OS disk N/A
Subscription ID baaa99b3-1d19-4c5e-90e1-39d55de5fc6e	Public IP address IPSpecialistvm-ip
	Private IP address 10.0.0.4
	Virtual network/subnet IPSpecialist-rg-vnet/default
	DNS name Configure

The virtual machine currently has one disk assigned to the machine which is the OS level disk

NAME	SIZE	STORAGE ACCO...	ENCRYPTION	HOST CACHING
IPSpecialistvm_OsDisk_1_addf931ff549...	127 GiB	Premium SSD	Not enabled	Read/write

Would you be charged for the compute cost of the virtual machine in its current state?

A. Yes

B. No

Answer – B

Explanation:

When the machine is in the Stopped (Deallocated) state, the compute costs are no longer charged to the customer.

The Microsoft documentation FAQ's on virtual machines mention the following

> If my deployed instance says "stopped," am I still getting billed?   ∧
>
> Maybe. If the status says "Stopped (Deallocated)," you're not being billed. If it says, "Stopped Allocated," you're still being billed for allocated virtual cores (not the software license itself). Full details on virtual machine states are available on the documentation page.

For more information on the pricing for Azure Windows virtual machines, please visit the below URL

https://azure.microsoft.com/en-us/pricing/details/virtual-machines/windows/

205. You have just setup a Windows virtual machine in Azure. The machine is currently in the stopped state. The details of the machine are given below

Resource group (change) IPSpecialist-rg	Computer name (start VM to view)
Status Stopped (deallocated)	Operating system Windows
Location Central US	Size Standard DS1 v2 (1 vcpus, 3.5 GiB memory)
Subscription (change) Pay-As-You-Go	Ephemeral OS disk N/A
Subscription ID baaa99b3-1d19-4c5e-90e1-39d55de5fc6e	Public IP address IPSpecialistvm-ip
	Private IP address 10.0.0.4
	Virtual network/subnet IPSpecialist-rg-vnet/default
	DNS name Configure

The virtual machine currently has one disk assigned to the machine which is the OS level disk

NAME	SIZE	STORAGE ACCO...	ENCRYPTION	HOST CACHING
IPSpecialistvm_OsDisk_1_addf931ff549...	127 GiB	Premium SSD	Not enabled	Read/write

Would you be charged for the underlying disks attached to the virtual machine in its current state?

A. Yes

B. No

Answer – A

Explanation:

You are always charged for the OS disk attached to the virtual machine

The Microsoft documentation FAQ's on virtual machines mention the following

General

Am I billed separately for local disk storage?

No. All new virtual machines have an operating system disk and a local disk (or "resource disk"). We don't charge for local disk storage. The operating system disk is charged at the regular rate for disks. See all virtual machines configurations.

For more information on the pricing for Azure Windows virtual machines, please visit the below URL

https://azure.microsoft.com/en-us/pricing/details/virtual-machines/windows/

206.   You have just setup a Windows virtual machine in Azure. The machine is currently in the stopped state. The details of the machine are given below

Resource group (change) IPSpecialist-rg	Computer name (start VM to view)
Status Stopped (deallocated)	Operating system Windows
Location Central US	Size Standard DS1 v2 (1 vcpus, 3.5 GiB memory)
Subscription (change) Pay-As-You-Go	Ephemeral OS disk N/A
Subscription ID baaa99b3-1d19-4c5e-90e1-39d55de5fc6e	Public IP address IPSpecialistvm-ip
	Private IP address 10.0.0.4
	Virtual network/subnet IPSpecialist-rg-vnet/default
	DNS name Configure

The virtual machine currently has one disk assigned to the machine which is the OS level disk

NAME	SIZE	STORAGE ACCO...	ENCRYPTION	HOST CACHING
IPSpecialistvm_OsDisk_1_addf931ff549...	127 GiB	Premium SSD	Not enabled	Read/write

Would you be charged for the private IP address assigned to the virtual machine in its current state?

A. Yes

B. No

Answer – B

Explanation:

You are only charged for the public IP addresses and not for the private IP addresses.

For more information on the pricing for IP addresses, please visit the below URL

https://docs.microsoft.com/en-us/azure/virtual-network/virtual-network-ip-addresses-overview-arm

207. A company has just setup an Azure subscription and an Azure tenant. They want to implement strict policies when it comes to the security of Azure resources. They want to implement the following requirements

- Ensure that the Virtual Machine Administrator team can only deploy virtual machines of a particular size.
- Ensure that the Virtual Machine Administrator team can only deploy virtual machines and their dependent resources.
- Ensure that no one can accidently delete the virtual machines deployed by the Virtual Machine Administrator team

Which of the following could be used to fulfil the below requirement?

"Ensure that the Virtual Machine Administrator team can only deploy virtual machines of a particular size"

A. Azure Role-Based Access Control

B. Azure Identity Protection

C. Azure Policies

D. Azure Locks

Answer – C

Explanation:

You can accomplish this with the help of policies. There is an in-built policy also available for this purpose

Allowed virtual machine SKUs
Policy definition

→ Assign   ✎ Edit definition   ⧉ Duplicate definition   🗑 Delete definition

Name	: Allowed virtual machine SKUs ⧉	Definition location : --	
Description	: This policy enables you to specify a set of virtual machine SKUs t...	Definition ID	: /providers/Microsoft.Authorization/policyDefinitions/cccc...
Effect	: Deny	Type	: Built-in
Category	: Compute	Mode	: Indexed

≪

Definition   Assignments (0)   Parameters

Option A is incorrect since this is used to given authorization to use Azure resources

Option B is incorrect since this is used to protect Azure AD identities

Option D is incorrect since this is used to protect Azure resources from users accidentally updating or deleting Azure resources

For more information on Azure policies, please visit the below URL

https://docs.microsoft.com/en-us/azure/governance/policy/overview

208.   A company has just setup an Azure subscription and an Azure tenant. They want to implement strict policies when it comes to the security of Azure resources. They want to implement the following requirements

- Ensure that the Virtual Machine Administrator team can only deploy virtual machines of a particular size.
- Ensure that the Virtual Machine Administrator team can only deploy virtual machines and their dependent resources.
- Ensure that no one can accidently delete the virtual machines deployed by the Virtual Machine Administrator team

Which of the following could be used to fulfil the below requirement?

"Ensure that the Virtual Machine Administrator team can only deploy virtual machines and their dependent resources."

A. Azure Role-Based Access Control
B. Azure Identity Protection
C. Azure Policies
D. Azure Locks

Answer – A

Explanation:

You can achieve this with Role-Based Access Control. You can deploy the Administrators to one group and just provide the role for virtual machine access.

The Microsoft documentation mentions the following

What is role-based access control (RBAC) for Azure resources?

09/11/2019 • 7 minutes to read • ● ● ● ●

Access management for cloud resources is a critical function for any organization that is using the cloud. Role-based access control (RBAC) helps you manage who has access to Azure resources, what they can do with those resources, and what areas they have access to.

RBAC is an authorization system built on Azure Resource Manager that provides fine-grained access management of Azure resources.

What can I do with RBAC?

Here are some examples of what you can do with RBAC:

- Allow one user to manage virtual machines in a subscription and another user to manage virtual networks
- Allow a DBA group to manage SQL databases in a subscription
- Allow a user to manage all resources in a resource group, such as virtual machines, websites, and subnets
- Allow an application to access all resources in a resource group

Option B is incorrect since this is used to protect Azure AD identities

Option C is incorrect since this is used to govern the resources in Azure

Option D is incorrect since this is used to protect Azure resources from users accidentally updating or deleting Azure resources

For more information on Azure Role based access control, please visit the below URL

https://docs.microsoft.com/en-us/azure/role-based-access-control/overview

209.   A company has just setup an Azure subscription and an Azure tenant. They want to implement strict policies when it comes to the security of Azure resources. They want to implement the following requirements

- Ensure that the Virtual Machine Administrator team can only deploy virtual machines of a particular size.
- Ensure that the Virtual Machine Administrator team can only deploy virtual machines and their dependent resources.
- Ensure that no one can accidently delete the virtual machines deployed by the Virtual Machine Administrator team

Which of the following could be used to fulfil the below requirement?

"Ensure that no one can accidently delete the virtual machines deployed by the Virtual Machine Administrator team"

A. Azure Role-Based Access Control

B. Azure Identity Protection

C. Azure Policies

D. Azure Locks

Answer – D

Explanation:

This can be achieved with the help of Azure Locks.

The Microsoft documentation mentions the following

Lock resources to prevent unexpected changes

05/14/2019 • 6 minutes to read • ⬤ ⬤ ⬤ ⬤ ⬤ +4

As an administrator, you may need to lock a subscription, resource group, or resource to prevent other users in your organization from accidentally deleting or modifying critical resources. You can set the lock level to **CanNotDelete** or **ReadOnly**. In the portal, the locks are called **Delete** and **Read-only** respectively.

- **CanNotDelete** means authorized users can still read and modify a resource, but they can't delete the resource.
- **ReadOnly** means authorized users can read a resource, but they can't delete or update the resource. Applying this lock is similar to restricting all authorized users to the permissions granted by the **Reader** role.

Option A is incorrect since this is used to given authorization to use Azure resources

Option B is incorrect since this is used to protect Azure AD identities

Option C is incorrect since this is used to govern the resources in Azure

For more information on Azure Locks, please visit the below URL

https://docs.microsoft.com/en-us/azure/azure-resource-manager/resource-group-lock-resources

210.   A company has just started using Azure. They have setup resources as part of their subscription. They want to get the current costs being incurred.

They decide to use Azure Cost Management to get this information

Would this fulfil the requirement?

A. Yes

B. No

Answer – A

Explanation:

Yes, this would give a cost breakdown for the resources being used in Azure.

An example is given below where you go to the Cost Analysis section in Cost Management.

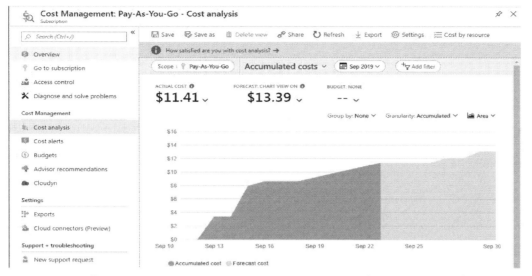

For more information on Azure Cost Management, please visit the below URL

https://docs.microsoft.com/en-us/azure/cost-management/overview

211. A company has just started using Azure. They have setup resources as part of their subscription. They want to get the current costs being incurred.

They decide to use the Pricing Calculator to get this information

Would this fulfil the requirement?

A. Yes

B. No

Answer - B

Explanation:

This tool is used as a cost estimation tool.

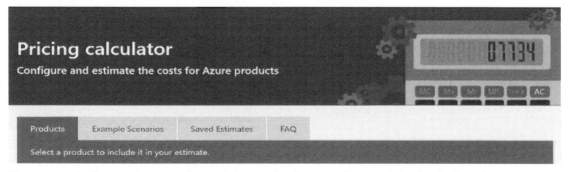

For more information on the pricing calculator, please visit the below URL

https://azure.microsoft.com/en-us/pricing/calculator/

212.   A company has just started using Azure. They have setup resources as part of their subscription. They want to get the current costs being incurred.

They decide to use the TCO calculator to get this information

Would this fulfil the requirement?

A. Yes

B. No

Answer - B

Explanation:

This is used to realize the costs when you move your current infrastructure to Azure.

For more information on the TCO calculator, please visit the below URL

https://azure.microsoft.com/en-us/pricing/tco/calculator/

213.   A company is currently planning on setting up resources as part of their Azure subscription. They are looking at different security options that can be used to secure their Azure environment.

Which of the following could be used for the following requirement?

"Provide the ability to restrict traffic into Azure virtual machines"

A. Azure Key Vault

B. Azure Network Security Groups

C. Azure Multi-Factor Authentication

D. Azure DDoS Protection

Answer - B

Explanation:

This can be accomplished with the help of Network Security Groups

The Microsoft documentation mentions the following

Security groups

07/26/2018 • 25 minutes to read • 🌑 🌑 🌑 🌑 🌑 +11

You can filter network traffic to and from Azure resources in an Azure virtual network with a network security group. A network security group contains security rules that allow or deny inbound network traffic to, or outbound network traffic from, several types of Azure resources. To learn about which Azure resources can be deployed into a virtual network and have network security groups associated to them, see Virtual network integration for Azure services. For each rule, you can specify source and destination, port, and protocol.

Option A is incorrect since this is used to store secrets, certificates and keys

Option C is incorrect since this is used to provide an extra level of security during user authentication

Option D is incorrect since this is used to protect against Distributed denial of service (DDoS) attacks

For more information on network security, please visit the below URL

https://docs.microsoft.com/en-us/azure/virtual-network/security-overview

214.   A company is currently planning on setting up resources as part of their Azure subscription. They are looking at different security options that can be used to secure their Azure environment.

Which of the following could be used for the following requirement?

"Provide an extra level of security when users log into the Azure Portal"

   A. Azure Key Vault
   B. Azure Network Security Groups
   C. Azure Multi-Factor Authentication
   D. Azure DDoS Protection

Answer – C

Explanation:

The extra level of security can be accomplished by providing a facility of Multi-Factor Authentication

The Microsoft documentation mentions the following

How it works: Azure Multi-Factor Authentication

The security of two-step verification lies in its layered approach. Compromising multiple authentication factors presents a significant challenge for attackers. Even if an attacker manages to learn the user's password, it is useless without also having possession of the additional authentication method. It works by requiring two or more of the following authentication methods:

- Something you know (typically a password)
- Something you have (a trusted device that is not easily duplicated, like a phone)
- Something you are (biometrics)

Option A is incorrect since this is used to store secrets, certificates and keys

Option B is incorrect since this is used to restrict traffic into and out of Azure virtual machines

Option D is incorrect since this is used to protect against Distributed denial of service (DDoS) attacks

For more information on multi-factor authentication, please visit the below URL

https://docs.microsoft.com/en-us/azure/active-directory/authentication/concept-mfa-howitworks

215. A company is currently planning on setting up resources as part of their Azure subscription. They are looking at different security options that can be used to secure their Azure environment.

Which of the following could be used for the following requirement?

"Provide a store that can be used to store secrets."

A. Azure Key Vault

B. Azure Network Security Groups

C. Azure Multi-Factor Authentication

D. Azure DDoS Protection

Answer – A

Explanation:

You can store secrets in the Azure Key Vault service.

The Microsoft documentation mentions the following

What is Azure Key Vault?

01/07/2019 • 4 minutes to read • ●●● ♨ ● +4

Azure Key Vault helps solve the following problems:

- **Secrets Management** - Azure Key Vault can be used to Securely store and tightly control access to tokens, passwords, certificates, API keys, and other secrets
- **Key Management** - Azure Key Vault can also be used as a Key Management solution. Azure Key Vault makes it easy to create and control the encryption keys used to encrypt your data.
- **Certificate Management** - Azure Key Vault is also a service that lets you easily provision, manage, and deploy public and private Secure Sockets Layer/Transport Layer Security (SSL/TLS) certificates for use with Azure and your internal connected resources.
- **Store secrets backed by Hardware Security Modules** - The secrets and keys can be protected either by software or FIPS 140-2 Level 2 validates HSMs

Option B is incorrect since this is used to restrict traffic into and out of Azure virtual machines

Option C is incorrect since this is used to provide an extra level of security during user authentication

Option D is incorrect since this is used to protect against Distributed denial of service (DDoS) attacks

For more information on the Azure Key Vault service, please visit the below URL

https://docs.microsoft.com/en-us/azure/key-vault/key-vault-overview

216.   A company is currently planning on setting up resources as part of their Azure subscription. They are looking at different security options that can be used to secure their Azure environment.

Which of the following could be used for the following requirement?

"Provide Protection against distributed denial of service attacks"

A. Azure Key Vault

B. Azure Network Security Groups

C. Azure Multi-Factor Authentication

D. Azure DDoS Protection

Answer – D

Explanation:

You can protect your environment from such attacks by using Azure DDoS Protection

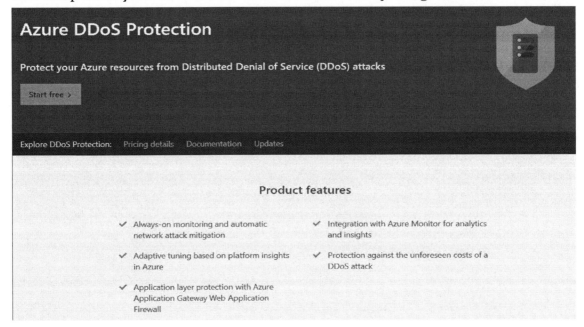

Option A is incorrect since this is used to store secrets, certificates and keys

Option B is incorrect since this is used to restrict traffic into and out of Azure virtual machines

Option C is incorrect since this is used to provide an extra level of security during user authentication

For more information on the Azure DDoS protection service, please visit the below URL

https://azure.microsoft.com/en-us/services/ddos-protection/

217. You are trying to understand the different cloud models. Which of the following are advantages of using the public cloud? Choose 2 answers from the options give below

A. Lower Capital Costs
B. Higher maintenance
C. High reliability
D. Higher Capital Costs

Answer – A and C

Explanation:

The advantages for using the public cloud is given in the Microsoft documentation

What is a public cloud?

Public clouds are the most common way of deploying cloud computing. The cloud resources (like servers and storage) are owned and operated by a third-party cloud service provider and delivered over the Internet. Microsoft Azure is an example of a public cloud. With a public cloud, all hardware, software, and other supporting infrastructure is owned and managed by the cloud provider. In a public cloud, you share the same hardware, storage, and network devices with other organizations or cloud "tenants." You access services and manage your account using a web browser. Public cloud deployments are frequently used to provide web-based email, online office applications, storage, and testing and development environments.

Advantages of public clouds:

- Lower costs—no need to purchase hardware or software, and you pay only for the service you use.

- No maintenance—your service provider provides the maintenance.

- Near-unlimited scalability—on-demand resources are available to meet your business needs.

- High reliability—a vast network of servers ensures against failure.

Since this is clearly given in the Microsoft documentation, all other options are incorrect

For more information on comparing the different models, please visit the below URL

https://azure.microsoft.com/en-us/overview/what-are-private-public-hybrid-clouds/

218.   You are trying to understand the different cloud models. Which of the following are advantages of using the private cloud? Choose 2 answers from the options give below

A. Less Flexibility

B. Better security

C. High scalability

D. Less costs

Answer – B and C

Explanation:

The advantages for using the private cloud is given in the Microsoft documentation

What is a private cloud?

A private cloud consists of computing resources used exclusively by one business or organization. The private cloud can be physically located at your organization's on-site datacenter, or it can be hosted by a third-party service provider. But in a private cloud, the services and infrastructure are always maintained on a private network and the hardware and software are dedicated solely to your organization. In this way, a private cloud can make it easier for an organization to customize its resources to meet specific IT requirements. Private clouds are often used by government agencies, financial institutions, any other mid- to large-size organizations with business-critical operations seeking enhanced control over their environment.

Advantages of a private clouds:

- More flexibility—your organization can customize its cloud environment to meet specific business needs.

- Improved security—resources are not shared with others, so higher levels of control and security are possible.

- High scalability—private clouds still afford the scalability and efficiency of a public cloud.

Since this is clearly given in the Microsoft documentation, all other options are incorrect

For more information on comparing the different models, please visit the below URL

https://azure.microsoft.com/en-us/overview/what-are-private-public-hybrid-clouds/

219.   You are trying to understand the different cloud models. Which of the following are advantages of using a hybrid cloud model? Choose 2 answers from the options give below

A. Better Control

B. Higher costs

C. More Flexibility

D. Less Maintenance

Answer – A and C

Explanation:

The advantages for using a hybrid cloud model is given in the Microsoft documentation

What is a hybrid cloud?

Often called "the best of both worlds," hybrid clouds combine on-premises infrastructure, or private clouds, with public clouds so organizations can reap the advantages of both. In a hybrid cloud, data and applications can move between private and public clouds for greater flexibility and more deployment options. For instance, you can use the public cloud for high-volume, lower-security needs such as web-based email, and the private cloud (or other on-premises infrastructure) for sensitive, business-critical operations like financial reporting. In a hybrid cloud, "cloud bursting" is also an option. This is when an application or resource runs in the private cloud until there is a spike in demand (such as seasonal event like online shopping or tax filing), at which point the organization can "burst through" to the public cloud to tap into additional computing resources.

Advantages of hybrid clouds:

- Control—your organization can maintain a private infrastructure for sensitive assets.
- Flexibility—you can take advantage of additional resources in the public cloud when you need them.
- Cost-effectiveness—with the ability to scale to the public cloud, you pay for extra computing power only when needed.
- Ease—transitioning to the cloud doesn't have to be overwhelming because you can migrate gradually—phasing in workloads over time.

Since this is clearly given in the Microsoft documentation, all other options are incorrect

For more information on comparing the different models, please visit the below URL

https://azure.microsoft.com/en-us/overview/what-are-private-public-hybrid-clouds/

220.   Is there a default spending limit when it comes to the spending limit for the Azure free account?

A. Yes

B. No

Answer – A

Explanation:

There is a credit of 200 USD which is assigned to the Azure Free account and is limited to the first 30 days the account is active. This acts as a spending limit. The Microsoft documentation mentions the following

Do I have to pay something after 30 days?

At the end of your first 30 days, you can continue using your free products after you upgrade your account to a pay-as-you-go pricing and remove the spending limit. If you stay within the service quantities included for free, you won't have to pay anything. The $200 free credit acts as a spending limit.

For more information on the common asked questions for the Azure Free account, please visit the below URL

https://azure.microsoft.com/en-us/free/free-account-faq/

221.   A company has just setup an Azure subscription. The company is planning on creating several resource groups. By creating additional resource groups, would the company incur additional costs?

A. Yes

B. No

Answer – B

Explanation:

Resource groups have no costs associate with them.

For more information on resource groups, please visit the below URL

https://docs.microsoft.com/en-us/azure/azure-resource-manager/resource-group-overview

222.   A company has just setup an Azure virtual private connection between their on-premise network and an Azure virtual network. Would the company need to pay additional costs if they transfer several gigabits of data from their on-premise network to Azure?

A. Yes

B. No

Answer – B

Explanation:

Data transfers to the Azure data center are free.

The Microsoft documentation mentions the following

Pricing details

Inbound data transfers

(i.e. data going into Azure data centers): **Free**

For more information on bandwidth pricing, please visit the below URL https://azure.microsoft.com/en-us/pricing/details/bandwidth/

223. A company has just setup an Azure virtual private network connection between their on-premise network and an Azure virtual network. The company expects around 10 GB worth of data transfer per month from Azure to their on-premise network. Would the company need to pay additional costs for this data transfer?

A. Yes
B. No

Answer – A

Explanation:

The company would need to pay additional costs for the data transfer.

A snippet from the Microsoft documentation mentions the following on data transfer prices

Outbound data transfers

(i.e. data going out of Azure data centers; zones refer to source region):

OUTBOUND DATA TRANSFERS	ZONE 1*
First 5 GB /Month [1]	Free
5 GB - 10 TB [2] /Month	$0.087 per GB
Next 40 TB (10 - 50 TB) /Month	$0.083 per GB
Next 100 TB (50 - 150 TB) /Month	$0.07 per GB

For more information on bandwidth pricing, please visit the below URL

https://azure.microsoft.com/en-us/pricing/details/bandwidth/

224. A company has a set of virtual machines defined in Azure. They want to find out which user shut down a particular virtual machine in the last 7 days. Which of the following can help the with this requirement?

A. Azure Advisor
B. Azure Event Hubs
C. Azure Activity Logs

D. Azure Service Health

Answer – C

Explanation:

You see all operations on all resources via the use of Azure Activity Logs

An example given below shows operations being logged against the Virtual Machine service.

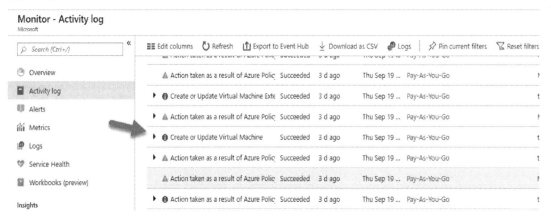

Since this is clear from the implementation, all other options are incorrect

For more information on Activity Logs, please visit the below URL

https://docs.microsoft.com/en-us/azure/azure-monitor/platform/activity-logs-overview

225.   A company wants to make use of an Azure service that can be used to store certificates. Which of the following could be used for storing certificates?

A. Azure Security Center

B. Azure Storage Account

C. Azure Key Vault

D. Azure Identity Protection

Answer – C

Explanation:

You can store certificates in the Azure Key vault service.

The Microsoft documentation mentions the following

What is Azure Key Vault?

01/07/2019 • 4 minutes to read • ⚫⚫⚫ 🔒 ⚫ +4

Azure Key Vault helps solve the following problems:

- **Secrets Management** - Azure Key Vault can be used to Securely store and tightly control access to tokens, passwords, certificates, API keys, and other secrets
- **Key Management** - Azure Key Vault can also be used as a Key Management solution. Azure Key Vault makes it easy to create and control the encryption keys used to encrypt your data.
- **Certificate Management** - Azure Key Vault is also a service that lets you easily provision, manage, and deploy public and private Secure Sockets Layer/Transport Layer Security (SSL/TLS) certificates for use with Azure and your internal connected resources.
- **Store secrets backed by Hardware Security Modules** - The secrets and keys can be protected either by software or FIPS 140-2 Level 2 validates HSMs

Option A is incorrect since this is used to increase the security posture of your resources defined in Azure

Option B is incorrect since this is used for object, file, table and queue storage

Option D is incorrect since this is used to protect Azure AD identities.

For more information on the Azure Key vault service, please visit the below URL

https://docs.microsoft.com/en-us/azure/key-vault/key-vault-overview

226.   A company wants to deploy a set of Azure Windows virtual machines. They want to ensure that the services on the virtual machines are still accessible even if a single data center goes down.

They decide to deploy the set of virtual machines using scale sets across availability zones

Would this fulfil the requirement?

A. Yes

B. No

Answer – A

Explanation:

Azure virtual machine scale sets let you create and manage a group of identical, load balanced VMs.

For more information on virtual machine scale sets, please visit the below URL

https://docs.microsoft.com/en-us/azure/virtual-machine-scale-sets/overview

227.   A company wants to deploy a set of Azure Windows virtual machines. They want to ensure that the services on the virtual machines are still accessible even if a single data center goes down.

They decide to deploy the set of virtual machines to two or more regions with the required traffic configurations in place

Would this fulfil the requirement?

    A. Yes
    B. No

Answer - A

Explanation:

For high availability of application, we can have VMs deployed in one or more regions. To know about how to work with this architecture do refer the following link.

https://docs.microsoft.com/en-us/azure/architecture/reference-architectures/n-tier/multi-region-sql-server

228.   A company wants to deploy a set of Azure Windows virtual machines. They want to ensure that the services on the virtual machines are still accessible even if a single data center goes down.

They decide to deploy the set of virtual machines to two or more availability zones.

Would this fulfil the requirement?

    A. Yes
    B. No

Answer – A

Explanation:

Yes, availability zones can be used in the case of data center wide failure.

The Microsoft documentation mentions the following

An Availability Zone in an Azure region is a combination of a **fault domain** and an **update domain**. For example, if you create three or more VMs across three zones in an Azure region, your VMs are effectively distributed across three fault domains and three update domains. The Azure platform recognizes this distribution across update domains to make sure that VMs in different zones are not updated at the same time.

With Availability Zones, Azure offers industry best 99.99% VM uptime SLA. By architecting your solutions to use replicated VMs in zones, you can protect your applications and data from the loss of a datacenter. If one zone is compromised, then replicated apps and data are instantly available in another zone.

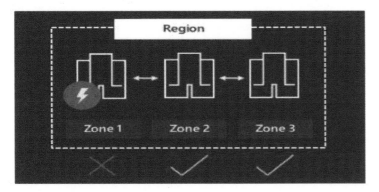

For more information on managing the availability of Azure windows virtual machines, please visit the below URL

https://docs.microsoft.com/en-us/azure/virtual-machines/windows/manage-availability

229.   A company wants to start using Microsoft Azure. They currently also have a private cloud setup. Would it be required for them to migrate their entire private cloud model to achieve a hybrid cloud model?

A. Yes

B. No

Answer – B

Explanation:

The Hybrid Cloud model combines both the public cloud and private cloud model. So, the company does not need to migrate their private cloud model to achieve the hybrid cloud model.

The Microsoft documentation mentions the following

What is a hybrid cloud?

A hybrid cloud is a computing environment that combines a public cloud and a private cloud by allowing data and applications to be shared between them. When computing and processing demand fluctuates, hybrid cloud computing gives businesses the ability to seamlessly scale their on-premises infrastructure up to the public cloud to handle any overflow—without giving third-party datacenters access to the entirety of their data. Organizations gain the flexibility and computing power of the public cloud for basic and non-sensitive computing tasks, while keeping business-critical applications and data on-premises, safely behind a company firewall.

For more information on the hybrid cloud model, please visit the below URL

https://azure.microsoft.com/en-in/overview/what-is-hybrid-cloud-computing/

230. A company wants to start using Microsoft Azure. Would using Azure help them scale the capacity of their on-premise setup?

A. Yes

B. No

Answer – A

Explanation:

Companies can indeed use public cloud providers such as Microsoft Azure to scale their on-premise setup.

The Microsoft documentation mentions the following

What is a hybrid cloud?

A hybrid cloud is a computing environment that combines a public cloud and a private cloud by allowing data and applications to be shared between them. When computing and processing demand fluctuates, hybrid cloud computing gives businesses the ability to seamlessly scale their on-premises infrastructure up to the public cloud to handle any overflow—without giving third-party datacenters access to the entirety of their data. Organizations gain the flexibility and computing power of the public cloud for basic and non-sensitive computing tasks, while keeping business-critical applications and data on-premises, safely behind a company firewall.

For more information on the hybrid cloud model, please visit the below URL

https://azure.microsoft.com/en-in/overview/what-is-hybrid-cloud-computing/

231. Is it possible to manage external partners using the "Business-to-Customer (B2C)" feature of Azure AD?

A. Yes

B. No

Answer – B

Explanation:

Microsoft Azure has an Identity service known as Microsoft Azure Active Directory. Using the "Business-to-Business (B2B)" feature of Azure AD you can manage your guest users and external partners, while maintaining control over your own corporate data.

Business-to-Business (B2B)	Manage your guest users and external partners, while maintaining control over your own corporate data. For more information, see Azure Active Directory B2B documentation.
Business-to-Customer (B2C)	Customize and control how users sign up, sign in, and manage their profiles when using your apps. For more information, see Azure Active Directory B2C documentation.

For more information on Identity solutions, please visit the below URL

https://docs.microsoft.com/en-us/azure/active-directory/fundamentals/active-directory-whatis

232.   You have to identify the right category for each of the following Azure Services

- Azure Kubernetes
- Azure Storage Accounts

Which of the following category does Azure Kubernetes come under?

    A. Software as a service
    B. Platform as a service
    C. Infrastructure as a service
    D. Hardware as a service

Answer – C

Explanation:

Azure Kubernetes comes as a "Infrastructure as a service".

Refer link : https://docs.microsoft.com/en-us/learn/modules/welcome-to-azure/3-tour-of-azure-services

Azure services

Here's a big-picture view of the available services and features in Azure.

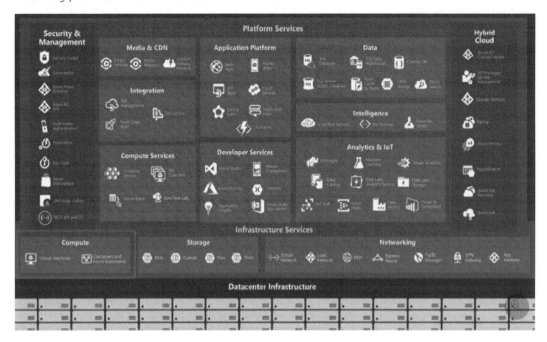

Since this is clearly mentioned in the documentation, all other options are incorrect

For more information on Infrastructure as a service, please visit the below URL

https://azure.microsoft.com/en-us/overview/what-is-iaas/

233. You have to identify the right category for each of the following Azure Services

- Azure Kubernetes
- Azure Storage Accounts

Which of the following category does Azure Storage Accounts come under?

A. Software as a service

B. Platform as a service

C. Infrastructure as a service

D. Hardware as a service

Answer – C

Explanation:

Azure Storage Accounts comes under the category of "Infrastructure as a service". Refer link:

https://docs.microsoft.com/en-us/learn/modules/welcome-to-azure/3-tour-of-azure-services

https://azure.microsoft.com/en-us/overview/what-is-iaas/

234.   A company wants to start deploying both Windows and Linux based Azure virtual machines. They also want to make use of availability zones for the underlying virtual machines. Could availability zones be used for both Windows or Linux Azure virtual machines?

A. Yes

B. No

Answer – A

Explanation:

If you look at the Microsoft documentation, they mention the support of Availability zones for both Windows and Linux based virtual machines

Services support by region

The combinations of Azure services and regions that support Availability Zones are:

	Americas				Europe		
	Central US	East US	East US 2	West US 2	France Central	North Europe	UK South
Compute							
Linux Virtual Machines	✓	✓	✓	✓	✓	✓	✓
Windows Virtual Machines	✓	✓	✓	✓	✓	✓	✓

For more information on availability zones, please visit the below URL

https://docs.microsoft.com/en-us/azure/availability-zones/az-overview

235.   A company wants to make use of availability zones in Azure. Can Availability zones be used to asynchronously replicate data across multiple regions?

A. Yes

B. No

Answer – B

Explanation:

Availability Zones are only specific to a region.

The Microsoft documentation mentions the following

An Availability Zone in an Azure region is a combination of a **fault domain** and an **update domain**. For example, if you create three or more VMs across three zones in an Azure region, your VMs are effectively distributed across three fault domains and three update domains. The Azure platform recognizes this distribution across update domains to make sure that VMs in different zones are not updated at the same time.

With Availability Zones, Azure offers industry best 99.99% VM uptime SLA. By architecting your solutions to use replicated VMs in zones, you can protect your applications and data from the loss of a datacenter. If one zone is compromised, then replicated apps and data are instantly available in another zone.

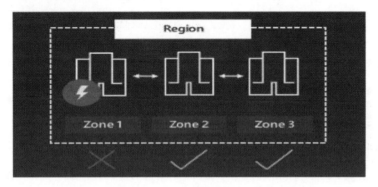

For more information on availability zones, please visit the below URL

https://docs.microsoft.com/en-us/azure/availability-zones/az-overview

236.   A company is planning on making use of Azure Service Health. Would the company administrator be able to view the health of the underlying Azure resources with the help of this service?

A. Yes

B. No

Answer – A

Explanation:

If you go to Service Health and Resource Health, you can see the health of your resources as shown below

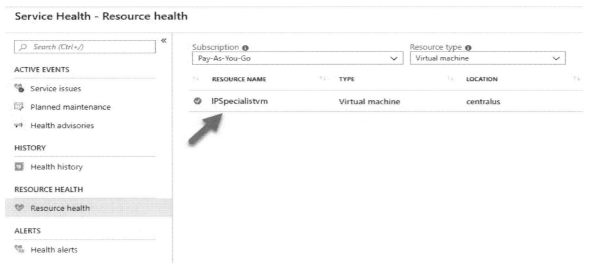

And if you go to Service Issues, you can see any issues with the underlying Azure Infrastructure

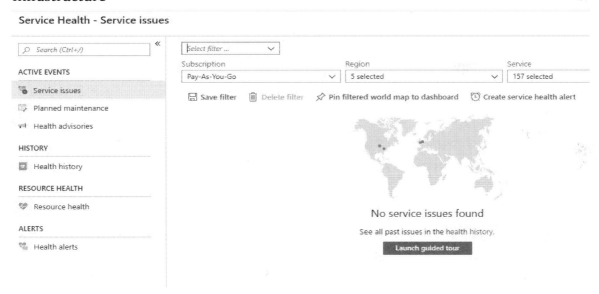

For more information on Azure Service Health, please visit the below URL

https://azure.microsoft.com/en-in/features/service-health/

237.   A company wants to make use of the Azure Service Health . Using this service, could the company administrator create a rule that sends alerts when an Azure service fails?

A. Yes

B. No

Answer – A

Explanation:

In Service Health, one can go to the "Health alerts" section and create a service health alert.

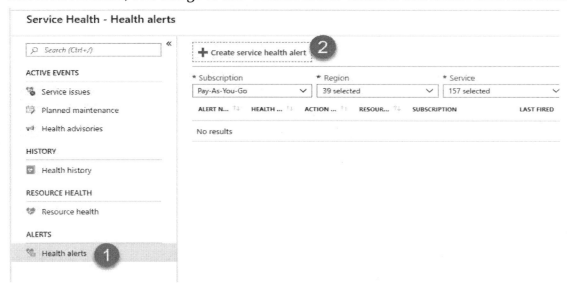

For more information on Azure Service Health, please visit the below URL

https://azure.microsoft.com/en-in/features/service-health/

238.   A company wants to make use of the Azure Service Health. Using this service, would the company administrator be able to prevent a service failure from affecting a select Azure virtual machine?

A. Yes

B. No

Answer – B

Explanation:

The Azure Service Health service is used to monitor the health of the underlying infrastructure that is used to host Azure based services. You cannot use this service to prevent the service failure of an Azure virtual machine.

If you want to increase the availability of your virtual machines, consider deploying the virtual machines across an availability set or an availability zone.

For more information on the Azure Service Health, please visit the following URL https://azure.microsoft.com/en-us/features/service-health/

239.   You have to identify the correct concept behind each of the following cloud service descriptions. Which of the following is the right concept behind the following description?

"A cloud service that can be accessed quickly by users over the Internet"

A. Fault Tolerance

B. Disaster Recovery

C. Dynamic Scalability

D. Low Latency

Answer – D

Explanation:

This is an example of low latency.

Following is a snippet from a Microsoft blog article

Latency is the new currency of the Cloud: Announcing 31 new Azure edge sites

Posted on August 27, 2019

 Yousef Khalidi, Corporate Vice President, Azure Networking

Providing users fast and reliable access to their cloud services, apps, and content is pivotal to a business' success.

The latency when accessing cloud-based services can be the inhibitor to cloud adoption or migration. In most cases, this is caused by commercial internet connections that aren't tailored to today's global cloud needs. Through deployment and operation of globally and strategically placed edge sites, Microsoft dramatically accelerates the performance and experience when you are accessing apps, content, or services such as Azure and Office 365 on the Microsoft global network.

Option A is incorrect since this is used to ensure a service is running even in the event of a service failure

Option B is incorrect since this is used to ensure a service is running even in the event of a catastrophic loss

Option C is incorrect since this is used to ensure a service is scalable even when the load on the service increases

For more information on the article, please visit the below URL https://azure.microsoft.com/en-us/blog/latency-is-the-new-currency-of-the-cloud-announcing-31-new-azure-edge-sites/

240.   You have the match the Azure Cloud Service benefit to the right description. Which of the following is the right Azure Cloud Service benefit that matches the following description?

"A cloud service that is able to perform as per the Service Level Agreement even after the load on the service increases"

A. Fault Tolerance

B. Disaster Recovery

C. Dynamic Scalability

D. Low Latency

Answer - C

Explanation:

This aligns itself with the concept of scalability

Azure has a service that helps in Autoscaling

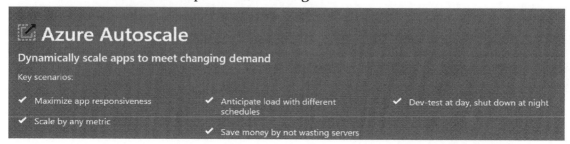

Option A is incorrect since this is used to ensure a service is running even in the event of a service failure

Option B is incorrect since this is used to ensure a service is running even in the event of a catastrophic loss

Option D is incorrect since this is used to ensure a service is quickly accessible to users over the Internet

For more information on Azure Autoscale, please visit the below URL

https://azure.microsoft.com/en-us/features/autoscale/

241.   You have the match the Azure Cloud Service benefit to the right description. Which of the following is the right Azure Cloud Service benefit that matches the following description?

"A cloud service that can be restored in the event of a catastrophic loss"

A. Fault Tolerance

B. Disaster Recovery

C. Dynamic Scalability

D. Low Latency

Answer - B

Explanation:

This term refers to disaster recovery.

Below is a snippet from the Microsoft documentation on the terminology

Failure and disaster recovery for Azure applications

04/10/2019 • 13 minutes to read •

Disaster recovery is the process of restoring application functionality in the wake of a catastrophic loss.

Your tolerance for reduced functionality during a disaster is a business decision that varies from one application to the next. It might be acceptable for some applications to be completely unavailable or to be partially available with reduced functionality or delayed processing for a period of time. For other applications, any reduced functionality is unacceptable.

Option A is incorrect since this is used to ensure a service is running even in the event of a service failure

Option C is incorrect since this is used to ensure a service is scalable even when the load on the service increases

Option D is incorrect since this is used to ensure a service is quickly accessible to users over the Internet

For more information on failure and disaster recovery, please visit the below URL

https://docs.microsoft.com/en-us/azure/architecture/reliability/disaster-recovery

242.   You have the match the Azure Cloud Service benefit to the right description. Which of the following is the right Azure Cloud Service benefit that matches the following description?

"A cloud service that remains available even if a fault occurs in the service"

   A. High Availability

   B. Disaster Recovery

   C. Dynamic Scalability

   D. Low Latency

Answer - A

Explanation:

This corresponds to "High Availability" or "Resiliency"

Below is a snippet from the Microsoft documentation on the terminology

https://docs.microsoft.com/en-us/azure/virtual-machines/workloads/sap/sap-high-availability-architecture-scenarios

High-availability architecture and scenarios for SAP NetWeaver

01/21/2019 • 11 minutes to read • 🔵🔵⚪⚪⚪ +1

Terminology definitions

High availability: Refers to a set of technologies that minimize IT disruptions by providing business continuity of IT services through redundant, fault-tolerant, or failover-protected components inside the *same* data center. In our case, the data center resides within one Azure region.

Option B is incorrect since this is used to ensure a service is running even in the event of a catastrophic loss

Option C is incorrect since this is used to ensure a service is scalable even when the load on the service increases

Option D is incorrect since this is used to ensure a service is quickly accessible to users over the Internet

For more information on designing reliable applications, please visit the below URL

https://docs.microsoft.com/en-us/azure/architecture/reliability/

243. A company needs to deploy a server named "ipspecialistserver" to the Azure cloud. The company's policy states that the server needs to be deployed on a separate network segment. Which of the following could be used to deploy the server to ensure that it's meet the company policy?

A. A separate resource group
B. A separate virtual network
C. A separate network interface for the server
D. A separate account for the server

Answer – B

Explanation:

If the server needs to be isolated, then consider deploying a new virtual network for the server.

The Microsoft documentation mentions the following

What is Azure Virtual Network?

06/19/2019 • 5 minutes to read • ⬡ ⬤ ⬤ ⬤ ⬤ +14

Azure Virtual Network (VNet) is the fundamental building block for your private network in Azure. VNet enables many types of Azure resources, such as Azure Virtual Machines (VM), to securely communicate with each other, the internet, and on-premises networks. VNet is similar to a traditional network that you'd operate in your own data center, but brings with it additional benefits of Azure's infrastructure such as scale, availability, and isolation.

All other options are invalid since they would not provide a means of isolation for the server.

For more information on virtual networks, please visit the below URL

https://docs.microsoft.com/en-us/azure/virtual-network/virtual-networks-overview

244. A company is planning on setting up a solution on the Azure platform. The solution has the following main key requirement

- Provide the ability to route traffic to backend virtual machines based on the attributes of an HTTP request

Which of the following would be best suited for this requirement?

A. Azure Data Lake Storage

B. Azure Application Gateway

C. Azure Storage Accounts

D. Azure SQL Data Warehouse

Answer – B

Explanation:

This can be achieved with the Azure Application Gateway.

The Microsoft documentation mentions the following

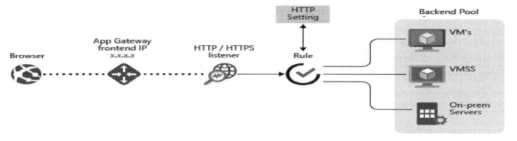

What is Azure Application Gateway?

05/31/2019 • 8 minutes to read • 🔵🔴🟤🟤

Azure Application Gateway is a web traffic load balancer that enables you to manage traffic to your web applications. Traditional load balancers operate at the transport layer (OSI layer 4 - TCP and UDP) and route traffic based on source IP address and port, to a destination IP address and port.

With Application Gateway, you can make routing decisions based on additional attributes of an HTTP request, such as URI path or host headers. For example, you can route traffic based on the incoming URL. So if `/images` is in the incoming URL, you can route traffic to a specific set of servers (known as a pool) configured for images. If `/video` is in the URL, that traffic is routed to another pool that's optimized for videos.

Since this is clearly mentioned in the documentation, all other options are incorrect

For more information on the Azure Application gateway service, please visit the below URL

https://docs.microsoft.com/en-us/azure/application-gateway/overview

245. A company is planning on setting up a solution on the Azure platform. The solution has the following main key requirement

- Provide a service that could help store objects that could be accessed from anywhere around the world via HTTP

Which of the following would be best suited for this requirement?

    A. Azure Data Lake Storage

    B. Azure Application Gateway

    C. Azure Storage Accounts

    D. Azure SQL Data Warehouse

Answer – C

Explanation:

This can be achieved with the Azure Storage Accounts service.

The Microsoft documentation mentions the following

Azure storage account overview

06/07/2019 • 14 minutes to read • ●●●● +3

An Azure storage account contains all of your Azure Storage data objects: blobs, files, queues, tables, and disks. The storage account provides a unique namespace for your Azure Storage data that is accessible from anywhere in the world over HTTP or HTTPS. Data in your Azure storage account is durable and highly available, secure, and massively scalable.

Since this is clearly mentioned in the documentation, all other options are incorrect

For more information on the Azure Storage Accounts service, please visit the below URL

https://docs.microsoft.com/en-us/azure/storage/common/storage-account-overview

246.   A company is planning on setting up a solution on the Azure platform. The solution has the following main key requirement

- Provide the ability to store petabytes of data
- Be able to run complex queries across the data

Which of the following would be best suited for this requirement?

    A. Azure Firewall

    B. Azure Application Gateway

    C. Azure Storage Accounts

    D. Azure Synapse

Answer – D

Explanation:

This can now be achieved with the help of the Azure Synapse service.

The Microsoft documentation mentions the following

What is Azure Synapse Analytics (formerly SQL DW)?

11/04/2019 • 2 minutes to read • 🌑🌑👤🌑🌑 +12

Azure Synapse is a limitless analytics service that brings together enterprise data warehousing and Big Data analytics. It gives you the freedom to query data on your terms, using either serverless on-demand or provisioned resources—at scale. Azure Synapse brings these two worlds together with a unified experience to ingest, prepare, manage, and serve data for immediate BI and machine learning needs

Azure Synapse has four components:

- SQL Analytics: Complete T-SQL based analytics – Generally Available
  - SQL pool (pay per DWU provisioned)
  - SQL on-demand (pay per TB processed) – (Preview)
- Spark: Deeply integrated Apache Spark (Preview)
- Data Integration: Hybrid data integration (Preview)
- Studio: Unified user experience. (Preview)

For more information on the Azure Synapse service, please visit the following URL

- https://docs.microsoft.com/en-us/azure/sql-data-warehouse/sql-data-warehouse-overview-what-is

247.   A company is planning on setting up a solution on the Azure platform. The solution has the following main key requirement

- Provide capabilities to perform Big Data analytics over data stored on Azure Blob storage

Which of the following would be best suited for this requirement?

- A. Azure Data Lake Storage
- B. Azure Application Gateway
- C. Azure Storage Accounts
- D. Azure SQL Data Warehouse

Answer – A

Explanation:

This can be achieved with the Azure Data Lake Storage service.

The Microsoft documentation mentions the following

Introduction to Azure Data Lake Storage Gen2

12/06/2018 • 4 minutes to read • ⬤ ⬤ ⬤ ⬤ ℛ +4

Azure Data Lake Storage Gen2 is a set of capabilities dedicated to big data analytics, built on Azure Blob storage. Data Lake Storage Gen2 is the result of converging the capabilities of our two existing storage services, Azure Blob storage and Azure Data Lake Storage Gen1. Features from Azure Data Lake Storage Gen1, such as file system semantics, directory, and file level security and scale are combined with low-cost, tiered storage, high availability/disaster recovery capabilities from Azure Blob storage.

Since this is clearly mentioned in the documentation, all other options are incorrect

For more information on the Azure Data Lake Storage service, please visit the below URL

https://docs.microsoft.com/en-us/azure/storage/blobs/data-lake-storage-introduction

248.   A company is planning on using Azure Information Protection. Which of the following is Azure Information Protection used for?

A. Azure Storage Accounts

B. Documents and Email Messages

C. Azure Active Directory Identities

D. Network Traffic

Answer – B

Explanation:

Azure Information Protection is used to protect documents and email Messages.

The Microsoft documentation mentions the following

What is Azure Information Protection?

06/21/2019 • 8 minutes to read • ⬤ ⬤ ⬤

> Applies to: _Azure Information Protection_

Azure Information Protection (sometimes referred to as AIP) is a cloud-based solution that helps an organization to classify and optionally, protect its documents and emails by applying labels. Labels can be applied automatically by administrators who define rules and conditions, manually by users, or a combination where users are given recommendations.

Since this is clearly mentioned in the documentation, all other options are incorrect

For more information on the Azure Information Protection, please visit the below URL

https://docs.microsoft.com/en-us/azure/information-protection/what-is-information-protection

249. A company wants to start using Azure. They want to have a declarative way to orchestrate the deployment of various resources types such as role assignments and policy assignments.

They decide to use Azure Information Protection

Would this fulfil the requirement?

A. Yes

B. No

Answer – B

Explanation:

This feature is used to secure email, documents and other sensitive data.

The Microsoft documentation mentions the following

Azure Information Protection

Better protect your sensitive information—anytime, anywhere

Control and help secure email, documents, and sensitive data that you share outside your company. From easy classification to embedded labels and permissions, enhance data protection at all times with Azure Information Protection—no matter where it's stored or who it's shared with.

For more information on the Azure Information Protection, please visit the below URL

https://azure.microsoft.com/en-us/services/information-protection/

250. A company wants to start using Azure. They want to have a declarative way to orchestrate the deployment of various resources types such as role assignments and policy assignments.

They decide to use Azure Blueprints

Would this fulfil the requirement?

A. Yes

B. No

Answer – A

Explanation:

This would fulfil the requirement

The Microsoft documentation mentions the following

Overview of the Azure Blueprints service

08/26/2019 • 7 minutes to read •

Just as a blueprint allows an engineer or an architect to sketch a project's design parameters, Azure Blueprints enables cloud architects and central information technology groups to define a repeatable set of Azure resources that implements and adheres to an organization's standards, patterns, and requirements. Azure Blueprints makes it possible for development teams to rapidly build and stand up new environments with trust they're building within organizational compliance with a set of built-in components -- such as networking -- to speed up development and delivery.

Blueprints are a declarative way to orchestrate the deployment of various resource templates and other artifacts such as:

- Role Assignments
- Policy Assignments
- Azure Resource Manager templates
- Resource Groups

For more information on the Azure Blueprints, please visit the below URL

https://docs.microsoft.com/en-us/azure/governance/blueprints/overview

251.   A company wants to start using Azure. They want to have a declarative way to orchestrate the deployment of various resources types such as role assignments and policy assignments.

They decide to use Azure AD Privileged Identity Management.

Would this fulfil the requirement?

A. Yes

B. No

Answer – B

Explanation:

This is used to manage, control and monitor access to critical resources in Azure.

The Microsoft documentation mentions the following

What is Azure AD Privileged Identity Management?

04/09/2019 • 4 minutes to read • ●●●●

Azure Active Directory (Azure AD) Privileged Identity Management (PIM) is a service that enables you to manage, control, and monitor access to important resources in your organization. This includes access to resources in Azure AD, Azure resources, and other Microsoft Online Services like Office 365 or Microsoft Intune.

For more information on the Azure privileged identity management, please visit the below URL

https://docs.microsoft.com/en-us/azure/active-directory/privileged-identity-management/pim-configure

252.   You just have started the deployment of an Azure Virtual machine to Azure. Where would you get a notification in the Azure portal on the completion of the deployment?

A. Using Link 1
B. Using Link 2
C. Using Link 3
D. Using Link 4

Answer – C

Explanation:

You will receive a notification in the Notification section.

Since this is clear from the implementation, all other options are incorrect

For more information on getting started with the Azure Portal, please visit the below URL

https://azure.microsoft.com/en-us/resources/videos/get-started-with-azure-portal/

253.   A company has just deployed a set of Azure virtual machines. They want their IT administrative team to get alerts whenever the CPU of the virtual machines goes beyond a certain threshold. Which of the following service could be used for this requirement?

A. Azure Advisor

B. Azure Security Center

C. Azure Monitor

D. Azure Active Directory

Answer – C

Explanation:

You can create alerts in Azure Monitor based on the virtual machine metrics

The Microsoft documentation mentions the following

What are alerts in Microsoft Azure?

Alerts proactively notify you when important conditions are found in your monitoring data. They allow you to identify and address issues before the users of your system notice them.

This article discusses the unified alert experience in Azure Monitor, which includes alerts that were previously managed by Log Analytics and Application Insights. The previous alert experience and alert types are called *classic alerts*. You can view this older experience and older alert type by selecting **View classic alerts** at the top of the alert page.

For more information on alerts in Azure Monitor, please visit the below URL

https://docs.microsoft.com/en-us/azure/azure-monitor/platform/alerts-overview

254.   A company is planning on using the Azure Database service. Could they use the Azure Database Migration service to migrate their current on-premise Microsoft SQL Server database to the Azure SQL database instance?

A. Yes

B. No

Answer – A

Explanation:

Yes, you can accomplish this with the Database Migration Service.

The Microsoft documentation mentions the following

What is Azure Database Migration Service?

05/31/2019 • 2 minutes to read • 🔵 🔴 🔵 🔴 🔵 +3

Azure Database Migration Service is a fully managed service designed to enable seamless migrations from multiple database sources to Azure data platforms with minimal downtime (online migrations).

Migrate databases to Azure with familiar tools

Azure Database Migration Service integrates some of the functionality of our existing tools and services. It provides customers with a comprehensive, highly available solution. The service uses the Data Migration Assistant to generate assessment reports that provide recommendations to guide you through the changes required prior to performing a migration. It's up to you to perform any remediation required. When you're ready to begin the migration process, Azure Database Migration Service performs all of the required steps. You can fire and forget your migration projects with peace of mind, knowing that the process takes advantage of best practices as determined by Microsoft.

For more information on the Database Migration Service, please visit the below URL

https://docs.microsoft.com/en-us/azure/dms/dms-overview

255.   Would the Azure Hybrid Benefit for Windows Server allow a customer to use his existing on-premises Windows Server licenses?

A. Yes

B. No

Answer – A

Explanation:

They can make use of the Azure Hybrid Benefit to get eligible discounts

The Microsoft documentation mentions the following

Azure Hybrid Benefit for Windows Server

04/22/2018 · 5 minutes to read · 👤👤👤👤😐 +6

For customers with Software Assurance, Azure Hybrid Benefit for Windows Server allows you to use your on-premises Windows Server licenses and run Windows virtual machines on Azure at a reduced cost. You can use Azure Hybrid Benefit for Windows Server to deploy new virtual machines with Windows OS. This article goes over the steps on how to deploy new VMs with Azure Hybrid Benefit for Windows Server and how you can update existing running VMs. For more information about Azure Hybrid Benefit for Windows Server licensing and cost savings, see the Azure Hybrid Benefit for Windows Server licensing page.

For more information on the Hybrid Benefit model, please visit the below URL

https://docs.microsoft.com/en-us/azure/virtual-machines/windows/hybrid-use-benefit-licensing

256.   A company is planning on using the Azure Cosmos DB service. Does the Cosmos DB service provide the ability to access different types of data stores such as Mongo DB and Cassandra?

A. Yes

B. No

Answer – A

Explanation:

Cosmos DB is a multi-model database.

The Microsoft documentation mentions the following

Azure Cosmos DB is Microsoft's globally distributed, multi-model database service. With a click of a button, Cosmos DB enables you to elastically and independently scale throughput and storage across any number of Azure regions worldwide. You can elastically scale throughput and storage, and take advantage of fast, single-digit-millisecond data access using your favorite API including SQL, MongoDB, Cassandra, Tables, or Gremlin. Cosmos DB provides comprehensive service level agreements (SLAs) for throughput, latency, availability, and consistency guarantees, something no other database service offers.

For more information on Azure Cosmos DB, please visit the below URL

https://docs.microsoft.com/en-us/azure/cosmos-db/introduction

257.   A company is planning on using the Azure Cosmos DB service. Would the company be able to deploy a custom software on the Azure Cosmos DB server?

A. Yes
B. No

Answer – B

Explanation:

Cosmos DB is a fully managed service. You don't get access to the underlying servers. One of the benefits of the Cosmos DB service is that you don't need to manage the underlying servers

Significant TCO savings

Since Cosmos DB is a fully managed service, you no longer need to manage and operate complex multi datacenter deployments and upgrades of your database software, pay for the support, licensing, or operations or have to provision your database for the peak workload. For more information, see Optimize cost with Cosmos DB.

For more information on Azure Cosmos DB, please visit the below URL

https://docs.microsoft.com/en-us/azure/cosmos-db/introduction

258.   A company is planning on using the Azure Cosmos DB service. Do you need to define a predefined schema for the tables on Cosmos DB?

A. Yes

B. No

Answer – B

Explanation:

Cosmos DB is based on a schema less design.

The Microsoft documentation mentions the following

No schema or index management

Keeping database schema and indexes in-sync with an application's schema is especially painful for globally distributed apps. With Cosmos DB, you do not need to deal with schema or index management. The database engine is fully schema-agnostic. Since no schema and index management is required, you also don't have to worry about application downtime while migrating schemas. Cosmos DB automatically indexes all data and serves queries fast.

For more information on Azure Cosmos DB, please visit the below URL

https://docs.microsoft.com/en-us/azure/cosmos-db/introduction

259.   A company has deployed a number of virtual machines to their Azure subscription. They want to know if there is any way to have a reduction in costs for running the virtual machines in Azure. Which of the following would help in this regard?

A. Virtual Machines

B. Advisor

C. Cost Management + Billing

D. Help + support

Answer – B

Explanation:

If you look at Azure Advisor, it can actually give you a purchase recommendation on how you can reduce costs when it comes to Virtual machines. Below is an example

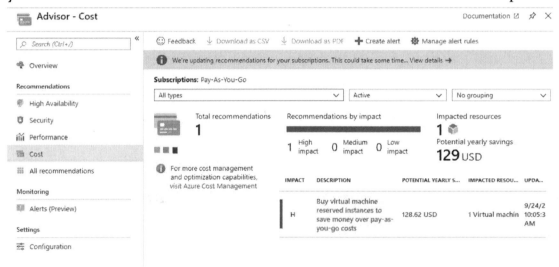

Since this is clear from the implementation, all other options are incorrect

For more information on Azure Advisor Cost Recommendations, please visit the below URL

https://docs.microsoft.com/en-us/azure/advisor/advisor-cost-recommendations

260.   A company has deployed an application which uses the Azure Web App service and the SQL database service. Currently the Azure Web App service has an SLA of 99.95% and that of the SQL database is 99.99%. Which of the following are used as availability metrics you would get from customers to understand the acceptability SLA for an application? Choose 2 answers from the options given below

A. Mean time to recover (MTTR)

B. Mean time between failures (MTBF)

C. Mean time to success (MTTS)

D. Mean time to failure (MTTF)

Answer – A and B

Explanation:

The 2 metrics are Mean time to recover (MTTR) and Mean time between failures (MTBF)

The Microsoft documentation mentions the following

Establish availability and recovery metrics

Create baseline numbers for two sets of metrics as part of the requirements process. The first set helps you determine where to add redundancy to cloud services and which SLAs to provide to customers. The second set helps you plan your disaster recovery.

Availability metrics

Use these measures to plan for redundancy and determine customer SLAs.

- **Mean time to recover (MTTR)** is the average time it takes to restore a component after a failure.
- **Mean time between failures (MTBF)** is the how long a component can reasonably expect to last between outages.

Since this clearly mentioned in the documentation all other options are incorrect

For more information on Architecture reliability requirements, please visit the below URL

https://docs.microsoft.com/en-us/azure/architecture/reliability/requirements

261.   A company has deployed an application which uses the Azure Web App service and the SQL database service. Currently the Azure Web App service has an SLA of 99.95% and that of the SQL database is 99.99%. Which of the following would be the SLA of the application?

A. 99.99%

B. 99.95%

C. 99.95% × 99.99% = 99.94%

D. (99.94% + 99.99%)/2 = 99.97%

Answer – C

Explanation:

Since there are 2 services as part of the application, we need to get the composite SLA.

The Microsoft documentation mentions the following

Composite SLAs

Composite SLAs involve multiple services supporting an application, each with differing levels of availability. For example, consider an App Service web app that writes to Azure SQL Database. At the time of this writing, these Azure services have the following SLAs:

- App Service web apps = 99.95%
- SQL Database = 99.99%

What is the maximum downtime you would expect for this application? If either service fails, the whole application fails. The probability of each service failing is independent, so the composite SLA for this application is 99.95% × 99.99% = 99.94%. That's lower than the individual SLAs, which isn't surprising because an application that relies on multiple services has more potential failure points.

For more information on Architecture reliability requirements, please visit the below URL

https://docs.microsoft.com/en-us/azure/architecture/reliability/requirements

262.   A company currently has deployed 2 virtual machines to Azure. The virtual machines would be hosting a web application. Users would be using the web application from the Internet. Would adding a VPN gateway to the solution increase the availability of the application?

A. Yes

B. No

Answer – B

Explanation:

The VPN gateway is used to create Virtual Private connections between the on-premise data center and an Azure network.

The Microsoft documentation mentions the following

What is VPN Gateway?

05/22/2019 • 13 minutes to read • 🌑 🌑 👤 🌑 🌑 +3

A VPN gateway is a specific type of virtual network gateway that is used to send encrypted traffic between an Azure virtual network and an on-premises location over the public Internet. You can also use a VPN gateway to send encrypted traffic between Azure virtual networks over the Microsoft network. Each virtual network can have only one VPN gateway. However, you can create multiple connections to the same VPN gateway. When you create multiple connections to the same VPN gateway, all VPN tunnels share the available gateway bandwidth.

For more information on the VPN gateway service, please visit the below URL

263. A company currently has deployed 2 virtual machines to Azure. The virtual machines would be hosting a web application. Users would be using the web application from the Internet. Would the use of an Azure Load balancer in the solution help increase the availability of the solution?

A. Yes
B. No

Answer – A

Explanation:

Yes, you can achieve higher availability for your applications by adding a Load balancer to the architecture.

The Microsoft documentation mentions the following

What is Azure Load Balancer?

01/11/2019 • 16 minutes to read • ⬤ ⬤ ⬤ ⬤ +9

With Azure Load Balancer, you can scale your applications and create high availability for your services. Load Balancer supports inbound and outbound scenarios, provides low latency and high throughput, and scales up to millions of flows for all TCP and UDP applications.

For more information on the Azure Load Balancer, please visit the below URL

https://docs.microsoft.com/en-us/azure/load-balancer/load-balancer-overview

264. A company currently has deployed 2 virtual machines to Azure. The virtual machines would be hosting a web application. Users would be using the web application from the Internet. Would it be better to deploy the virtual machines as part of an Azure Virtual machine scale set to increase the availability of the application?

A. Yes
B. No

Answer – A

Explanation:

Yes, you can achieve higher availability for your applications by adding the virtual machines to a virtual machine scale set.

The Microsoft documentation mentions the following

What are virtual machine scale sets?

05/21/2018 • 3 minutes to read • ⬤ ⬤ ⬤ ⬤ ⬤

Azure virtual machine scale sets let you create and manage a group of identical, load balanced VMs. The number of VM instances can automatically increase or decrease in response to demand or a defined schedule. Scale sets provide high availability to your applications, and allow you to centrally manage, configure, and update a large number of VMs. With virtual machine scale sets, you can build large-scale services for areas such as compute, big data, and container workloads.

For more information on Virtual Machine scale sets, please visit the below URL

https://docs.microsoft.com/en-us/azure/virtual-machine-scale-sets/overview

265.   A company wants to make use of a data store on the Azure platform. The data store would be used to store user profile information related to an application.

The company decides to create an Azure Storage Account and then use the Blob service to store the user profile data.

Is this the ideal service to use for this requirement?

A. Yes

B. No

Answer – B

Explanation:

This service is normally used to store objects.

The Microsoft documentation mentions the following

About Blob storage

Blob storage is designed for:

- Serving images or documents directly to a browser.
- Storing files for distributed access.
- Streaming video and audio.
- Writing to log files.
- Storing data for backup and restore, disaster recovery, and archiving.
- Storing data for analysis by an on-premises or Azure-hosted service.

For more information on Azure Blob storage, please visit the below URL

https://docs.microsoft.com/en-us/azure/storage/blobs/storage-blobs-introduction

266. A company wants to store application related user data onto Azure. They decide to create an Azure Storage Account. They then decide to use the File service to store the user data.

Is this the ideal service for storage of user related data?

A. Yes

B. No

Answer – B

Explanation:

This service is used when you want have files that can be accessed via the SMB 3.0 and HTTPS protocol.

The Microsoft documentation mentions the following

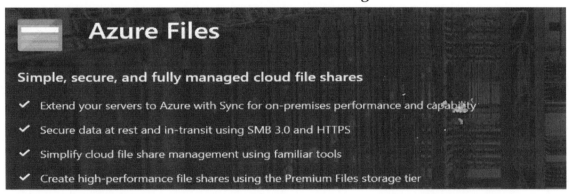

For more information on the Azure File service, please visit the below URL

https://azure.microsoft.com/en-us/services/storage/files/

267. A company wants to store application related user data onto Azure. They decide to create an Azure Storage Account. They then decide to use the Table service to store the user data.

Is this the ideal service for storage of user related data?

A. Yes

B. No

Answer – A

Explanation:

Yes, this is the ideal service for storing application related user data.

The Microsoft documentation mentions the following

Azure Table storage is a service that stores structured NoSQL data in the cloud, providing a key/attribute store with a schemaless design. Because Table storage is schemaless, it's easy to adapt your data as the needs of your application evolve. Access to Table storage data is fast and cost-effective for many types of applications, and is typically lower in cost than traditional SQL for similar volumes of data.

You can use Table storage to store flexible datasets like user data for web applications, address books, device information, or other types of metadata your service requires. You can store any number of entities in a table, and a storage account may contain any number of tables, up to the capacity limit of the storage account.

For more information on Azure Table storage, please visit the below URL

https://docs.microsoft.com/en-us/azure/cosmos-db/table-storage-overview

268.   You have defined an Azure virtual network in a resource group named "ipspecialist-rg". The name of the virtual network is "ipspecialist-rg-vnet". You plan to assign a policy which specifies that virtual networks are not an allowed resource type in the resource group "ipspecialist-rg". What happens to the existing network once the policy is applied?

A. The network is automatically deleted

B. The network is moved to a different resource group

C. The network resources would become a read-only resource

D. The virtual network would continue to exist as it is

Answer – D

Explanation:

Azure policies would just show the resources as a non-compliant resource as shown below. As such the resource would remain as it is.

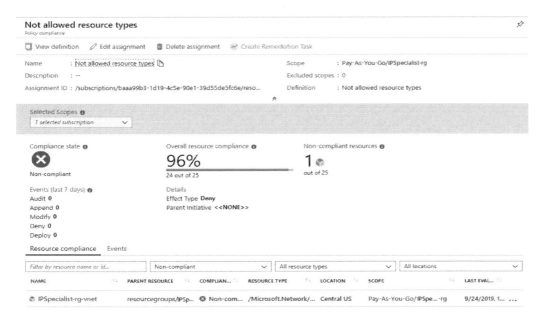

Not allowed resource types
Policy compliance

📄 View definition　✏️ Edit assignment　🗑️ Delete assignment　🔲 Create Remediation Task

Name	: Not allowed resource types 📄	Scope	: Pay-As-You-Go/IPSpecialist-rg
Description	: --	Excluded scopes : 0	
Assignment ID	: /subscriptions/baaa99b3-1d19-4c5e-90e1-39d55de5fc6e/reso...	Definition	: Not allowed resource types

Selected Scopes ⓘ

`1 selected subscription`

Compliance state ⓘ	Overall resource compliance ⓘ	Non-compliant resources ⓘ
❌	**96%**	**1** 📦
Non-compliant	24 out of 25	out of 25

Events (last 7 days) ⓘ
Audit 0
Append 0
Modify 0
Deny 0
Deploy 0

Details
Effect Type **Deny**
Parent Initiative <<NONE>>

Resource compliance　Events

| Filter by resource name or id... | Non-compliant ⌄ | All resource types ⌄ | All locations ⌄ |

NAME	PARENT RESOURCE	COMPLIAN...	RESOURCE TYPE	LOCATION	SCOPE	LAST EVAL...
🔷 IPSpecialist-rg-vnet	resourcegroups/IPSp...	❌ Non-com...	/Microsoft.Network/...	Central US	Pay-As-You-Go/IPSpe...-rg	9/24/2019, 1... ...

Since this is clear from the implementation, all other options are incorrect

For more information on Azure policies, please visit the below URL

https://docs.microsoft.com/en-us/azure/governance/policy/overview

269.　　You have defined a resource group named "ipspecialist-rg". The resource group currently has the following resources

NAME ↑↓	TYPE ↑↓	RESOURCE GROUP ↑↓
☐ 🔷 IPSpecialist-rg-vnet	Virtual network	IPSpecialist-rg
☐ 🖥️ IPSpecialistvm	Virtual machine	IPSpecialist-rg
☐ 🖼️ IPSpecialistvm-ip	Public IP address	IPSpecialist-rg
☐ 🛡️ IPSpecialistvm-nsg	Network security group	IPSpecialist-rg
☐ ⬛ IPSpecialistvm138	Network interface	IPSpecialist-rg
☐ 💾 IPSpecialistvm_OsDisk_1_addf931ff520444....	Disk	IPSPECIALIST-RG

The resource group has the following lock in place

➕ Add　☁️ Subscription　🔄 Refresh

LOCK NAME	LOCK TYPE	SCOPE	NOTES		
grouplock	Delete	🔲 IPSpecialist-rg		✏️ Edit	🗑️ Delete

Would you be able to stop the virtual machine "ipspecialistvm" if it was in the running status?

A. Yes

B. No

Answer – A

Explanation:

Here the lock is a delete type lock. You can still work with resources in the resource group. You only can't delete resources in the resource group.

The Microsoft documentation mentions the following on Azure Locks

Lock resources to prevent unexpected changes

05/14/2019 • 6 minutes to read • 🟢 🔵 ⚫ 🔴 ⚫ +4

As an administrator, you may need to lock a subscription, resource group, or resource to prevent other users in your organization from accidentally deleting or modifying critical resources. You can set the lock level to **CanNotDelete** or **ReadOnly**. In the portal, the locks are called **Delete** and **Read-only** respectively.

- **CanNotDelete** means authorized users can still read and modify a resource, but they can't delete the resource.
- **ReadOnly** means authorized users can read a resource, but they can't delete or update the resource. Applying this lock is similar to restricting all authorized users to the permissions granted by the **Reader** role.

For more information on Azure Locks, please visit the below URL

https://docs.microsoft.com/en-us/azure/azure-resource-manager/resource-group-lock-resources

270. You have defined a resource group named "ipspecialist-rg". The resource group currently has the following resources

NAME ↑↓	TYPE ↑↓	RESOURCE GROUP ↑↓
⟨⋯⟩ IPSpecialist-rg-vnet	Virtual network	IPSpecialist-rg
🖥 IPSpecialistvm	Virtual machine	IPSpecialist-rg
🖼 IPSpecialistvm-ip	Public IP address	IPSpecialist-rg
🛡 IPSpecialistvm-nsg	Network security group	IPSpecialist-rg
▦ IPSpecialistvm138	Network interface	IPSpecialist-rg
💾 IPSpecialistvm_OsDisk_1_addf931ff520444....	Disk	IPSPECIALIST-RG

The resource group has the following lock in place

✚ Add	🔒 Subscription	↻ Refresh				
LOCK NAME	**LOCK TYPE**	**SCOPE**	**NOTES**			
grouplock	Delete	(⟨⟩) IPSpecialist-rg			✎ Edit	🗑 Delete

Would you be able to create a new resource in the resource group "ipspecialist-rg"?

A. Yes

B. No

Answer - A

Explanation:

Here the lock is a delete type lock. You can still create resources in the resource group. You only can't delete resources in the resource group.

The Microsoft documentation mentions the following on Azure Locks

Lock resources to prevent unexpected changes

05/14/2019 • 6 minutes to read • 🟢 🔵 ⚫ 🟠 👥 +4

As an administrator, you may need to lock a subscription, resource group, or resource to prevent other users in your organization from accidentally deleting or modifying critical resources. You can set the lock level to **CanNotDelete** or **ReadOnly**. In the portal, the locks are called **Delete** and **Read-only** respectively.

- **CanNotDelete** means authorized users can still read and modify a resource, but they can't delete the resource.

- **ReadOnly** means authorized users can read a resource, but they can't delete or update the resource. Applying this lock is similar to restricting all authorized users to the permissions granted by the **Reader** role.

For more information on Azure Locks, please visit the below URL

https://docs.microsoft.com/en-us/azure/azure-resource-manager/resource-group-lock-resources

271.   You have defined a resource group named "ipspecialist-rg". The resource group currently has the following resources

NAME ↑	TYPE ↑	RESOURCE GROUP ↑
‹··› IPSpecialist-rg-vnet	Virtual network	IPSpecialist-rg
IPSpecialistvm	Virtual machine	IPSpecialist-rg
IPSpecialistvm-ip	Public IP address	IPSpecialist-rg
IPSpecialistvm-nsg	Network security group	IPSpecialist-rg
IPSpecialistvm138	Network interface	IPSpecialist-rg
IPSpecialistvm_OsDisk_1_addf931ff520444....	Disk	IPSPECIALIST-RG

The resource group has the following lock in place

✚ Add   🔒 Subscription   ↻ Refresh

LOCK NAME	LOCK TYPE	SCOPE	NOTES		
grouplock	Delete	🖼 IPSpecialist-rg		✏ Edit	🗑 Delete

Would you be able to delete the virtual machine "ipspecialistvm"?

A. Yes

B. No

Answer – B

Explanation:

Since we have a delete lock in place at the resource group level, you will not be able to delete any resource in the resource group.

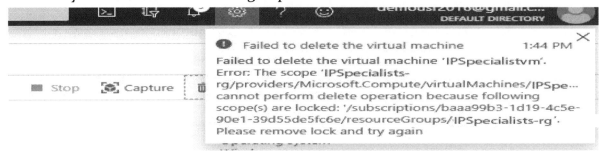

For more information on Azure Locks, please visit the below URL

https://docs.microsoft.com/en-us/azure/azure-resource-manager/resource-group-lock-resources

272.   A company wants to start using Azure. They want to deploy a number of resources to their Azure subscription. They want to be informed if the costs of Azure resources goes beyond a certain threshold. Which of the following can help achieve this?

A. Create an alert in Azure Monitor

B. Create a budget in Azure Cost Management

C. Create an alert in Azure Advisor

D. Create a cost tag for the resource group

Answer – B

Explanation:

You can create a budget and get a notification if the costs are going beyond the budget.

The Microsoft documentation mentions the following

Tutorial: Create and manage Azure budgets

09/09/2019 • 6 minutes to read • ⬤ ⬤ ⬤ ⬤

Budgets in Cost Management help you plan for and drive organizational accountability. With budgets, you can account for the Azure services you consume or subscribe to during a specific period. They help you inform others about their spending to proactively manage costs, and to monitor how spending progresses over time. When the budget thresholds you've created are exceeded, only notifications are triggered. None of your resources are affected and your consumption isn't stopped. You can use budgets to compare and track spending as you analyze costs.

Cost and usage data is typically available within 8-12 hours and budgets are evaluated against these costs every four hours. Email notifications are normally received within 12-16 hours.

Since this is clearly mentioned in the Microsoft documentation, all other options are incorrect

For more information on Azure budgets, please visit the below URL

https://docs.microsoft.com/en-us/azure/cost-management/tutorial-acm-create-budgets

273.   You are planning on creating an Azure Free Account. Which of the following is correct when it comes to the Azure Free Account? Choose 2 answers from the options given below

A. You get free access to all services for 12 months.

B. You get USD 200 worth of credit that you can spend during the first 30 days of sign-up

C. After the 30-day period of USD 200 worth of credit is over, for continuous usage, you need to convert to a Pay-As-You-Go account.

D. You only need to have a valid mobile number to sign-up for the account

Answer – B and C

Explanation:

The following is mentioned in the Microsoft documentation to support the correct options

Option A is incorrect because you don't get free access to ALL products, just the popular ones.

Option D is incorrect because you also need to have a credit card or Microsoft account in hand.

For more information on the Azure Free Account, please visit the below URL

https://azure.microsoft.com/en-us/free/free-account-faq/

274. A company wants to deploy a custom solution available from a vendor onto Azure. Where should the company search to see if the solution is already readily available to be deployed?

A. In Azure Security Center

B. In the Azure Marketplace

C. In Azure Advisor

D. In Azure Monitor

Answer – B

Explanation:

You can look for already solutions in the Azure Marketplace

The Microsoft documentation mentions the following

What is Azure Marketplace?

Azure Marketplace provides access and information on solutions and services available from Microsoft and our partners. Customers (IT professionals and developers) can discover, try to buy cloud software solutions built on or built for Azure. Our catalog of 8,000+ listings provides Azure building blocks, such as Virtual Machines (VMs), APIs, Azure apps, Solution Templates and managed applications, SaaS apps, containers, and consulting services.

Since this is clearly mentioned in the Microsoft documentation, all other options are incorrect

For more information on the Azure Marketplace, please visit the below URL

https://docs.microsoft.com/en-us/azure/marketplace/marketplace-faq-publisher-guide

Printed in Great Britain
by Amazon

86965765R00140